Amish Life through a Child's Eyes

by

Alma Hershberger

Photos by John M. Zielinski

To my family

Copyright © by Alma Hershberger

All rights reserved. No part of this publication may be reproduced, stored in a retrieval system, or transmitted, in any form or by any means, electronic, mechanical, photocopying, recording, or otherwise, without written permission of the copyright owner.

Published by
Amish Taste Cooking Company,
Box 375
Danville, Ohio 43014,
in collaboration with
Amish Heritage Publications.

Autographed copies can be obtained by writing Alma Hershberger at P.O. Box 375, Danville, Ohio 43014. Phone (614) 599-7072. Information about ordering other books about the Amish can be obtained from her or Amish Heritage Publications, P.O. Box 2660, Iowa City, IA 52244.

Typeset by Small Town America Publications
P.O. Box 2660
Iowa City, IA 52244

Table of Contents

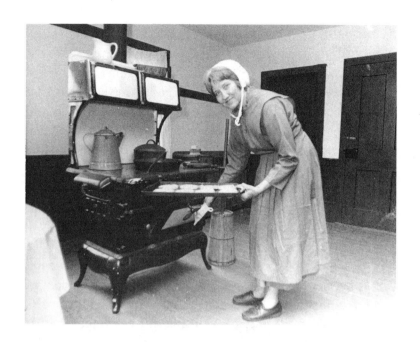

Preface

Alma (Troyer) Hershberger, is a little lady who has worn many hats since taking off her Amish bonnet at the age of 14. Mrs. Hershberger was one of the co-founders of the Der Dutchman restaurants in Ohio, and mother of three. She has been a guest chef demonstrating Amish cooking, a lecturer on Amish life for schools and on the radio and television. She acted in a pageant, and found time to write two cookbooks, with a new one, "Amish Taste Cooking: Simplified Step by Step" even now going to the printers. She also wrote a book called "Alphabet in Amish Life".

Now as we see her on the following pages she is pre-
pared to put on her Amish clothes once again in order to
demonstrate what Amish life is like. We see Alma in the Amish
Home, a beautifully done presentation of Amish life on what
used to be a small Amish farm near Walnut Creek, Ohio on
Route 515. Here Alma portrays Amish life as her mother once
lived it with woodburning cookstove and woodburning stove
in the parlor, the only source of heat in most Amish homes.

Although Alma and part of her family left the Amish
more than 25 years ago, she still has three brothers and one
sister, along with her father who remained Amish. This was
out of a total of nine children.

Alma still speaks with the trace of the German accent
that is her heritage. She spoke nothing but German when she
went to kindergarten in Buchanan County, Iowa in the 1940's
where a new community of Amish is still growing. She had
to go to a public school where she had to speak English.

Unfortunately the form of German the Amish speak is
a much altered dialect from modern German. It is a spoken,
not written language, although even today Alma is likely to
sprinkle her English with Dutch.

Throughout her life Alma staunchly defends the Amish
way of life, while not hesitating to point out some of its hypo-
crises. Recently Alma spoke to a farmer who was bemoaning
the fact that he now had an Amish neighbor. "Those dumb
Dutchman..." Alma waded into the conversation bristling.
"Don't you know that wherever the Amish move in the land
values soon go up? You should be thanking him for raising the
value of your land." She was referring to the fact that Amish
farming techniques enrich the land and within five years of
taking over so called worn out land, they have often doubled

the per acre yield over the "modern farmer". Amish farm techniques were admired by all in colonial America. It was the early Amish and Mennonites who helped transform the Lancaster area into what became known as the "Breadbasket of America" for its production of wheat and grains. In the 1870's it was once again the Amish and Mennonites who helped transform the Kansas prairies into the Kansas wheatlands, another breadbasket. Today the Amish are seeking more and more farmland across America where their techniques of manuring and composting help to restore land that was once thought to be exhausted.

Today in America there are more and more Amish buggies to be seen in new states as the exploding Amish population looks for new farmland and prepares to revitalize small town America. They need a lively small town only a brief buggy ride away from their farms.

To promote understanding of the Amish life, Alma Hershberger is offering herself as a bridge of understanding- not only sharing her life in written words but offering to speak on radio, television and in the schools of America. Her address and phone number can be found on the copyright page of this book.

Alma Hershberger explains the Amish way of life at the Amish Home on Route 515, near Walnut Creek, Ohio. She will speak to groups and give cooking demonstrations upon request.

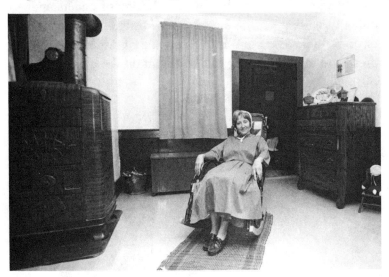

Top: Amish father and sons mend fence and do chores.
Bottom: It was time for early Spring plowing along the Amish
Highway between Oelwein and Independence, Iowa.

Alma stands beside an Amish buggy in front of the school she wrote about attending near Oelwein, Iowa. She talked to the teacher at Triumph School during her visit.

Alma revisited the barn where she and her brothers and sisters played as children. Bottom photo is the home of her relatives still living in Buchanan County, Iowa.

Two of Alma's brothers get the horse and buggy ready.
Other than the photo of Alma as a child, this is the only
photo of the people mentioned in Amish Life Through
a Child's Eyes. All the other photos were taken by John
M. Zielinski, and represent Amish people illustrating
themes from the book. They were taken all across the
country, from Kansas to Pennsylvania.

Introduction

The Amish are people who take pride in their country and their freedom and take great interest in their farmland. The Amish lead a very plain life and live quietly in their own community. They believe in God. However, their religion is based on their tradition. They believe you are to be different from the world. Tradition is handed down from the past. You should do as your forefathers did. My mother always said, "Love your enemies"(Luke 6:35) and "Judge not others; then you won't be judged".(Luke 6:37)

My family is in twenty-five different states throughout the United States and Canada. Those states are Alabama, Arizona, Colorado, Delaware, Florida, Georgia, Illinois, Indiana, Iowa, Kansas, Kentucky, Maryland, Michigan, Minnesota, Missouri, New York, Ohio, Oklahoma, Pennsylvania, South Carolina, Tennessee, Texas, Virginia, and Wisconsin. The Amish are the fastest growing ethnic group in America today.

In doing the cookbooks that I have done, *Art of Amish Cooking* and *Alma's Amish Kitchen*, I have called on practically every Amish community across the country.

My story is one of ten thousand stories that could be told of Amish life in America today. In looking at my cousin's family book, I note that one in Texas has ten children. Anyone who thinks that the Old Order Amish are dying out are mistaken. They are actually exploding across the American land.

My family takes great interest in their heritage. They compiled a book going from our ancestor of 1763 to 1989. My mother's family book was compiled by Laura (Stutzman) Gingerich in 1979 and titled *Stutzman History Steps from Switzerland*. Another book was done by Polly Stoll of Aylmer, Ontario. My father's family book was

17

compiled by Mr. and Mrs. Levi Mast in May 1975. In the beginning it gave a little history.

The stars fell in 1833. My father's family book explained how the men and women awoke about eleven o'clock one night. They awoke their children to see a display that alarmed them. They thought the whole atmosphere was burning. The children were too young to understand and weren't afraid.

The night was as quiet as death. There wasn't a breath of wind. The stars fell in the manner of a heavy snow falling. Every star, large and small, was falling straight down. They couldn't see any of them hit the earth. The believers and nonbelievers thought this was the end of the world. They all got down on their knees and prayed. The display lasted for two hours.

History is passed on from our ancestors to families of today. My uncles compiled a book titled *The Troyer Team*. This book tells how their family moved to Oklahoma when they were young boys. In the depression, Grandpa lost their farm. The boys built a wagon, and Grandpa made a map of the way to Oklahoma. The boys each had a wagon with a team of horses. Since there was no money to move, they followed each other, like a wagon train. One wagon hauled grain. One had the household goods, and another wagon had the wagon wheel grease, the blankets, and the food that Grandma had made for them to eat on the eight-day trip. This trip was made from Kansas to Oklahoma.

This is my story of my life growing up in Iowa. A lot of Amish children growing up in Amish settlements would have a story to tell.

My family decided to move to Iowa in January of 1943. The story of *Amish Life through a Child's Eyes* is the history of my Amish family's experience form 1943 to 1951. My family didn't realize that their trials and tribulations were just beginning for the entire family when they made the move to Iowa. In 1951 my family decided to leave the hard life in Iowa. This was Mother's way to keep the family together.

When I was an eleven-year-old Amish girl, a vision flashed through my head. It was as if a voice was saying, *Write a book about your life in Iowa.* I asked, "Write a book about Iowa? But how? I don't even know how to begin." As the time went by, I could never forget that moment.

Some years later, I talked to my family about the book and asked them what they thought of the idea. They didn't say too much at first. Later, my oldest sister asked me not to write about our life. I asked her why. She said, "You still have brothers with the Amish, and it may make hard feelings. You wouldn't want to do that, would you?" She didn't understand that this idea had nothing to do with my family still being Amish.

I want everyone who reads this book to realize that I love my brothers and sisters dearly and I'm proud of each and every one of them. Remember, the Amish community of Buchanan County was unique. And this family was a unique one among the Amish. Once you start to read the story, you'll see what I mean.

I kept asking myself, *Why do I feel that I am supposed to write this book? Why me? I must write it even if it's against my family's wishes.* My book began to be an obsession with me.

This is a true story. You may find that my writing is a little backward, as I am an Amish woman. But really it's correct; it's just that you English people are a little backward with your language.

The Move to Iowa

About the first thing I remember was the move from Oklahoma to Iowa. I was three years old and had four brothers and two sisters when we packed up and moved. I was the sixth child born to my mother, and I was named after my aunt, Alma Troyer. At that time, our family consisted of: William Glen, age 11, born November 23, 1932; Levi, age 9, born January 9, 1934; Susan, age 8, born August 18, 1935; Polly, born March 30, 1937 died April 2, 1937; Daniel, age 5, born August 14, 1938; Alma, age 3, born February 25, 1940; Elizabeth, age 2, born April 6, 1941; and Henry Jr., age 6 months, born July 30, 1942.

We moved in the winter, after the crops had been harvested in the fall. We moved by train. Most Amish did move by train because it was convenient. At the time, my older brother William was eleven years old. He was an ambitious boy with light brown hair and blue eyes. He and my father herded the livestock into cattle cars. All our household goods and personal belongings were crated and moved in boxcars. Mother, the girls, and the younger children rode in the coach while Father and the older brothers rode in the cattle car.

I can't remember much about that trip, only that the train went very fast and a man in a blue suit with a funny cap checked with Mom to make sure everything was all right. Mom's brother, Uncle Judas, and her sister, Aunt Pauline, both farmers, had come, along with Uncle Henry, to meet us at the train station in Independence, Iowa. Uncle Henry was Mom's brother, too, and he was a minister in the Amish church.

According to our family history book, my father's Amish ancestor Samuel Mueller arrived in America, from Canton Berns, Switzerland, in a ship with Capt. Charles

21

Smith. The ship landed in Philadelphia on November 1, 1763, with 193 passengers.

My mother's ancestor Jacob Ammann came to America from Switzerland in 1749. Jacob Ammann was known to be one of the founders of the Amish settlement in Hertzel, Pennsylvania.

The Amish families that left Switzerland were looking for a free country where they might live and worship according to their own beliefs, without restrictions.

However, at that time none of the Amish men were bishops. Through mail, Mr. Jacob Ammann, from the Old Country, was nominated as their first bishop. Traditionally, when the Amish need a preacher, the Amish members nominate several men from the congregation on one Sunday and then in two weeks they take the same number of songbooks and place a piece of paper in one of them. Whoever receives the book with the paper is the chosen one.

The Amish hold church service in their homes. When the congregation grows too large for their houses, they divide the congregation. They pinpoint the center of the Amish community and draw a line from west to east and south to north. The ones who live in the western section belong to the West Church, those in the east belong to the East Church, and so on. This rule is used all over the United States. In some communities you may find a Middle Church necessary when the four "directional" congregations grow too large.

In Buchanan County, Iowa, we had three churches. My family belonged to the West Church. Church services started at nine o'clock; and lasted until one in the afternoon. Dinner was served after the service and consisted of peanut butter and jelly on bread, with pickles and red beets placed on a large platter, so everyone could reach and help themselves. The people in our new church were all very nice to us, but their ways were different from what we were used to.

In Iowa, the men's church shirts were made of all white cotton material. The style was open just enough to get the head through, with long sleeves and about three hooks and eyes sewed on instead of buttons to close it. The white shirt was worn with a black suit and vest. The boys' hats were made out of black wool with extra wide brims. The watergate of the pants had buttons instead of a zipper. (Watergate is a nickname for the slacks opening, what the English call the fly.)

The Oklahoma clothes didn't fit into the Iowa style because they were made to conform to the body. Iowans' clothes are looser. To the Iowa Amish eyes, Oklahoma clothes were immodest.

The church people told Mom and Dad they could change their clothing style as we wore our clothes out and months after we moved to Iowa, we were told we would have to get rid of our Oklahoma clothes and dress as the Iowans did. The material was to be a solid dark color and made of cotton.

Father was able to rent a vacant farm about four miles from the one we bought. The farm we bought needed some work to get it ready for us to move in, so we lived on a rented farm temporarily. Dad wanted our new home done for us before it was time to work in the fields.

When we pulled up to the new house, everything felt so strange. I wished Mom could have told Dad to turn around and take us back home. The vacant farmhouse had a big front porch with lots of glass windows, and if I stood on my tippy-toes, I could just about see out. On our first day at the new house, many Amish people came to help Mom unpack. They stayed until it was time to do their evening chores. So we made a lot of friends that day.

There are no other denominations in Buchanan County except for the English people. According to the Amish, the English people in Buchanan were the only people who don't speak the Amish language.

I slept with my two other sisters. Elizabeth, who is fourteen months younger than I, was a slender girl with black hair. Susan, who was eight, has blond hair and fair complexion, with blue eyes. She thought she should have her own bed. Mom said sleeping together was a good way of keeping warm, so we didn't really mind it so much.

There was a lot of work to be done at the new farm, so I came to miss my father and brothers very much. They were gone before I woke up in the morning, and we didn't get to see them until suppertime. Stories at the supper table were always fun, because the boys would tell us how things were coming on the new farm. We were also looking forward to moving in, not realizing that the trials and tribulations were just beginning for the family.

Father's Accident

The Wapsipinicon River, with woods on both sides, ran across Buchanan County from the southeast to the northwest, through our ninety-four-acre farm. It ran along the far south side of our land, running east and west and making a turn at the far west end, and running north. The river was about a quarter-mile from the house and outbuildings.

Behind the outbuildings we had a natural running creek traveling southeast like a snake through the barnyard and woods, emptying into the river. The river and the creek had its low and high banks.

Dad and the boys had about four miles to go back and forth from the new farm. On the first day of March 1944, the ground was still covered with snow. Dad hitched a team of horses to the old box bobsled and loaded the two-man timber saw and ax. He left with my brothers to go to the new farm to cut firewood, using methods that had not changed since the days of the early American settlers.

While Dad and my brothers were cutting firewood, the sun came out and the snow disappeared, leaving the roads covered with patches of ice. When Dad and the boys had the sled loaded and came out of the shaded woods and into the sun, the snow was too far gone to try to take the heavily loaded sled over the melted roads. They parked the loaded sled and unhitched the team of draft horses.

Dad lifted the two boys, age ten and eleven, up on one horse and jumped on the other horse. They started back home with the team, riding by holding onto the harness. They had traveled for one mile when they came to a farm at a curve. Father's horse slipped on the ice-covered road and fell on top of my father. Father's horse tried to get up but slipped again. With Father still astride, the horse went back down again, falling on Father's leg and thumping Father's head down on the icy road. The boys immediately jumped off their horse and ran to the house for assistance. They helped Father to the house and called the doctor. Father was the type that didn't believe in X-rays or hospitals. He was just too stubborn to go.

By the first of April, we were able to move to our new farm, but Father's leg continued to give him trouble. His physical problems seemed to be changing his mental attitude. He went into a depressed state of mind. He claimed there were men in the woods coming after him. Then he began showing suicidal tendencies.

One day my brother William was on his horse ready to go after the cows when Dad stopped him and said, "I'll go." My brother gave him the horse, and Dad went to the woods. However, he didn't come back. Finally, Mom decided to send the boys down into the woods to see if they could find him. Soon the boys came running back and reported, "Dad's sitting down on the riverbank with his shoes off, hanging his feet in the river. He's looking into the water and saying, 'Look at the little devils in there. Little devils are all over. It's full of little devils.'" Later Dad came back without the cows. Then Brother went after the cows. Another day, Sister Susan was standing at the windmill when she saw Father walking toward her from the barn. Unaware of our father's disturbed state of mind, she walked over and hugged his leg and started to say something. "Shh?" he said. "Everybody will hear you."

"Who will hear me?"

"Everyone in the world will hear you."

She looked around, but didn't see anyone. As a nine-year-old child, she couldn't understand that statement and was silent. Soon she left in silence.

Mother knew she had to do something, but what and how was a problem. She tried to cope with Dad and wouldn't say anything to anyone about what was happening until one Sunday when our entire family was humiliated by Father's strange behavior.

26

Typically, on Sunday morning, our family had a brief devotion and prayer meeting at home before leaving for church. This one Sunday morning when it was time to have prayer, Dad started from the beginning of the prayer book that he used. The book was in German, and we were on our knees for an hour. Our time was running out, and we were going to be late for church services.

Mom realized what was happening, so she interfered "Henry , you can't go through that whole book; we'll be late." He wouldn't stop. Soon Mom got to her feet and said,"Come, children, eat your breakfast." We all followed Mom quietly to the kitchen, leaving Dad still on his knees. Soon he followed.

After breakfast, Mom suggested."We are an hour late; why don't we skip church today?"

"No, we're going to church," Dad replied.

We went to church, and how embarrassed the family was to arrive at midmorning. Church started at 9:00 A.M. and was over at 1:00 P.M. After service, Mom tried to explain and had a long talk with her brother, Uncle Judas, about Dad's attitude.

Uncle Judas went to Independence to see what could be done. Independence was the closest city, about fifteen miles from the farm. When Uncle Judas returned, my mother was faced with some very difficult decisions to make. She began to realize that if she hoped to find help for my father, she would be forced to seek this help outside our Amish community. Amish people value their independence and do not believe in involving governmental agencies in their lives. My mother also knew she was three months pregnant. How could she manage her family without the help of her husband if he was not at home?

Time passed for a while without any major incidents. My sister Annie was born and was still a tiny infant when a terrifying event occurred in my mother's life. One night after she went to bed, she sensed something coming toward her and ducked her head. She felt my father's fist going into the pillow, hitting the headboard and barely missing her head.

Another day, Father hitched the horse to the buggy and said,"I have to go to Joe Miller's." Joe lived across the river and was the bishop of our church. When Father arrived there, he didn't know what he wanted anymore.

Uncle Paul and Aunt Pauline's farm was on the east side of our farm. We were next-door neighbors about one fourth-mile away. They began to realize that something was wrong with my father. Sometimes Dad would take off running into the woods and then he would be on Aunt Pauline's doorstep. They would ask him."What are you doing?" He wouldn't know what he was doing there or what he wanted.

Uncle Judas and Aunt Pauline wanted Mom to take Dad to a doctor, but there was no way Dad would go. As I said before, he was too stubborn. However, Uncle Judas heard about a special doctor in Waterloo, Iowa. So he came to see Mom. He asked,"Would you be interested in taking Henry to see a special doctor?"

"*Ja.*"

"But how are you going to get him to go?

"I don't know."

"Why don't we ask Sister Pauline and her husband Paul if they would go and the three couples would go together? Pretend that everyone needs a check-up?"

"I'll go see if they agree."

"All right."

Soon Uncle Judas came back and told Mom that the others would go. They made arrangements for the three couples to go see the doctor. When they arrived, Uncle Judas and his wife Tilly went in first. This gave Uncle Judas the opportunity to explain Henry's ways to the doctor before Dad and Mom went in. Then Paul and Pauline were called in. When it was time for Mom and Dad, the doctor wanted to examine Dad.

Dad said,"She's the one that's sick; nothing's wrong with me. You check her."

They all left disappointed. Uncle Paul was still afraid of his mentally disturbed brother-in-law living on a farm next to his. Now what could they do?

By now, Mom had the new baby, Annie. Mom knew she had to watch Dad to make sure he didn't hurt one of the children or even himself. Tension grew very strong in our home. Sometimes my father would get up throughout the night and Mom would have to check him. The guns were put away, along with the sharp knives.

More and more, my father was losing touch with reality. In Iowa, we had red fox season and the men would get together during this time for fox hunting in the evening. Out of season, Dad sent Brother Levi to the neighbors and to Uncle Judas, to tell them that he wanted them to come over to go fox hunting. Everyone but Dad, of course, realized it was not red fox season.

Uncle Judas went again to call the doctor to plead with him to come out and check Henry .

"Is he sick in bed?" the doctor asked, knowing about Dad's condition.

"No."

"Well, if you can't make him come in and if he's not sick in bed, there is nothing I can do for him."

Uncle Judas had to go to the police about the problem. They said they would pick Dad up at the house.

The neighbors came over that night, and Uncle Judas notified the church congregation that Henry would be picked up that night. The neighbor men were out fox hunting, and they were called in. We had company. Uncle Judas informed Mom of what he had done. The church members and family came to lend their moral support.

After supper, as the women were doing the dishes, I saw a car coming down the road. I watched the car until it passed the house. The car pulled up in the driveway, turned around and stopped.

Two men in plainclothes stepped out of the vehicle and asked the boys in the yard, "Is this where Henry Troyer lives?"

"*Ja*," was the reply from the group.

The men came to the house, and someone opened the door for them to step inside.

"Mom, two guys are here," I said.

29

"Is Henry Troyer here?" one man asked.

"Yes," Mother answered

"Where is he?"

"He's in the living room."

The man look in and asked,"Which one is he?"

"The one with the little one sleeping on his lap."

The men went to the door and asked,"Is Henry here?"

"Yeah," he answered, standing up to place the baby on the daybed and walking toward them.

"We came to pick you up; will you go with us?"

"Yeah," he answered and led the way to their car without saying anything to anyone as he left.

The gentleman asked Mom if she had a way to get to Independence in the morning. If she didn't, they would come and pick her up and bring her back again. She had to go in to sign some papers to transfer Dad to the state hospital in the morning. She thanked the gentleman and told them that she would be there. They asked her not to visit my father at the new hospital until they notified her that it would be all right. The gentleman left the house to join his friend, who was waiting in the car with Dad.

The room was silent after the man left. I think everyone was surprised that my father left voluntarily. None of the guests seemed to know what to say.

Then one of the Amish men broke the silence in the quiet room,"Well, we'd better head for home. Katie, if you need help, let us know."

Uncle Judas spoke."I'll have my boys help you with the farm," he said.

When all the guests had gone, Mother said,"We'd better go to bed so we can get up in the morning."

We children were sad that Father had to leave. We all obeyed in silence, hoping there would be help for Father in Independence. We all thought he would be well and back home again soon.

Visitation

Three months dragged by. Mother was finally permitted to visit the hospital to see Dad and check on his progress. His condition would vary from visit to visit. Sometimes he was quite rational, and other times he wasn't too good.

As time passed, the little ones wouldn't eat their food. Mother tried to coax, but they would only sit at their place crying, asking for their father. The older ones had to brace themselves and looked at us younger ones with courage to be strong. At times like this, it was always silent, except for the one that cried. Our wordless eye contacts did most of our talking across the table for us. Sometimes we had to swallow twice to stay in control. It was hard to explain to the ones who were too young to understand. We all longed for our father to be home.

Mother contacted the hospital and made arrangements to bring the little ones in for visitation. Since all the children were minors, she had to get permission from the hospital before bringing them in to visit.

On the Saturday morning of the first scheduled visit, Mother told the older boys to get the family team and buggy ready for the trip to the state hospital. "We are going to see your father today," she said. It was the first trip to Independence for the young ones. We were in store for a new adventure.

We had traveled about ten miles when Mother pulled into a farmer's yard. A friendly middle-aged farmer's wife, with brown hair and a bib apron, walked out to greet us. Mother stepped from the buggy and met her halfway. Mother asked, "May we give our horses some water, please?"

"Sure! Just pull over to the windmill by the water tank."

Mother thanked her, and we watered our horses and continued on toward Independence.

We came to a racetrack with rows of bleachers. There were men exercising horses pulling two-wheeled carts around the track. We children really admired the beautiful sight. After we passed the track, we came to our first paved street as we entered the city limits. With two horses pulling the rig, we passed along Main Street. The children's eyes were open wide. The city and its sights were a novel experience for young Amish children.

Past the center of town, Mother turned left onto a side street. We noticed a large building high on a hilltop.

I said,"Oh! Mom, look at the big beautiful place up there."

"*Ja*, that's where your father's at."

"Oh! Really? It's beautiful!"

"*Ja*, it is."

She turned onto the paved drive that cut through a huge yard surround by beautiful trees on either side. When we reached the building at the end of the drive, a gentleman came out to meet us. He reached to clutch the horses by the reins while we stepped out of the buggy. Mother thanked him and found a spot to tie the horses to a fence post. Like a mother hen with her baby chicks behind her, my mother led us into the building.

Oh, how excited we were to see Father again. I remember, when we went inside, how I admired those large hallways with the open stairways to the second floor.

Mother stopped at the desk."We are here to see Henry Troyer," she said.

They sent us to the second floor. As we went upstairs, I noticed the beautiful chandeliers hanging from the ceiling. To a young Amish girl, this was a most beautiful sight. At the top of the stairs, we turned left through double doors to the first room on the right. In the small room was a large window, a bed, a dresser, and a chair. This was Dad's room. Someone went to the recreation room to fetch him as we waited with excitement. Soon Dad came in an took a chair across from Mother while we children sat on his bed opposite them.

We visited for a while, and, of course, Henry Jr., who was a toddler, became restless. He climbed up on the bed and walked to the window to look outside. Father stood up and quickly grabbed him off the bed and spanked him. Henry Jr. cried. Mother took him in her arms and sat him on her lap. Soon Mother said,"We have to go." She feared we were upsetting Father.

On our way home, we stopped at the same farm to give our horses some water. No one had much to say all the way home.

A couple of weeks later, Mother received word that Dad had left the hospital on his own. They had found him downtown. When they picked him up, he had bought a poison of some kind. Since then, they were keeping him locked up for a while in a ward. Later we received word he was doing better again and was able to move around the hospital grounds.

We visited him several more times at the hospital. One time he was sitting out in the yard on a bench under a shade tree while most of the others were inside watching television. Another time when we arrived they said he wasn't in.

Mother asked,"Where is he?"

"He's out helping make hay."

They called him in from the field on a radio. We walked to the barnyard fence. We could see Dad coming toward us in good spirits. We visited for a while and left.

The visits with Dad helped Mother cope with the pressure when the children missed their father and wanted him home.

One summer day we received word that Dad was released from the hospital for two weeks for a vacation at home. When we received word, Mother directed,"William and Levi, you hide the gun."

"Where do you want us to hide it?" William asked. Levi listened attentively.

"Where would be a good place?" she asked.

Levi suggested,"In the haymow."

"No, it has to be where he won't go. He may help throw hay down and find it there."

33

"Should we put it upstairs under out bed?"

"No, he surely would find it in the house. It can't be in the house or barn."

Everybody was nervous and started to think hard. Hiding the gun in the buggy shed or at the blacksmith's wasn't a good idea.

Someone suggested,"How about the ditch across the road?" Everybody agreed.

Someone asked,"What if he goes after the mail?"

"We'll put it in the deep part where the weeds are, and we'll have to make sure we go after the mail before he does."

When we picked up Dad, they told Mom,"Now if you have any trouble, you may bring him back before his two weeks are up." We were happy that Dad was coming home, but we were all nervous, not knowing how he really was going to be for two weeks. We had already had him home several times just for the weekend, and he was always ready to go back to his second home at the end of the weekend. We had to watch him very closely, and it was a strain on all of us.

On the first day, Dad was glad to be home. He was in good spirits. The second day, he walked to the kerosene barrel and saw the lock on it. He started to talk to himself and giggle. He walked to the blacksmith shop to get the hammer and came back and knocked the lock off with one strike. Then he picked up a tin can and filled it with kerosene.

Mom and we children were standing inside the house watching Dad. We were astonished to see him break the lock so easily, and we were all concerned. He destroyed it as fast as a blink of an eye.

Mom expressed ,"Oh, na!"

One of the children asked,"What is he going to do with the kerosene?"

Then there was dead silence. Dad started to walk toward the barn.

Mom said,"Stay here," and she followed him. When she caught up with him, he was out behind the barn.

She asked,"What are you going to do, Henry ?"

Dad looked at her and brought the can up to his mouth to take a drink. Mom quickly reached out and knocked it out of his hand, spilling it to the ground. He started back to get more, talking and laughing to himself. He filled the can and went to the house.

Mom stated firmly,"If you don't put that down, I'll take you back where I picked you up at." He looked at her and she commanded him,"Give the can to me." He handed it to her peacefully. We all were silent and scared for what might happen. We all knew he had more strength than we all had put together. After this incident, he was quiet again for that day.

Several days later, Dad asked,"Where is the gun?"

"The gun isn't here," Mom answered.

Dad walked out to the road toward the mailbox. We all watched in silence and fear.

Levi went outside quickly and said,"Dad, I got the mail already." Dad didn't say anything.

Levi repeated,"Dad, I got the mail."

Dad stopped and looked at him, then answered,"Oh, you got the mail already."

"*Ja.*"

Then Dad started to talk again and walked in the road, looking across the fields. We didn't dare say any more, for Father might suspect something. We could relax again when Father walked away without seeing the gun.

When my mother was only thirty-two years old, I noticed her hair was almost all white.

One afternoon it was quiet around the house. Mom' checked to see where Dad and we children were. She saw Dad standing at the northeast corner of the barn with a long lead pipe in his hand. He was beating at something, but she couldn't see what. She looked to see where we children were, but couldn't see any of us around. She was breathless. I can only imagine what horrid thoughts went through her head. She quickly walked around the northwest side of the barn to see what Dad was beating at. She saw we were standing in fear by the creek behind the barn watching him beating the corner post.

With relief, she said softly, "Kinder"(children), getting our attention. We looked. She said, "Come this way." We all went to her while keeping an eye on Dad.

Mom decided she couldn't keep an eye on Dad for two weeks. The horse and buggy were hitched up to take Dad back to his second home.

This was hard on Mom, as well as for the rest of the family. We felt guilty taking my dad back early. We also hated being without a man in charge in our family. It was up to us all to do the farming and keep us in food and clothes.

Two years later, the doctors asked Mother to transfer my father to Davenport State Hospital for testing. Davenport was much farther from our home, but the doctors thought Dad would get better treatment there. They wanted to see what was causing his condition, because they still didn't know. They had given him as much treatment as they were able to with the knowledge they had.

Mother made arrangements to have Dad transferred. Two weeks after he was transferred, we received word that the doctors wanted to talk to Mother. They thought they might have found what was causing the problem.

Mother stated, "Good! Maybe we can get this problem solved."

We couldn't believe the doctors knew already what was wrong. We were excited. Mother left early in the morning, and all the children stayed at home, anxiously awaiting word of what the problem was and what could be done.

Chores were done and supper was on the table, but Mother wasn't home yet. We didn't wait on her, because we didn't know what time she would be home. While we were at the table, she opened the door. She gave us her friendly smile and came inside.

"What did they have to say about Dad?" William asked.

"Well, they claim he received a pinched nerve in his lower back, a nerve that is connect to his spinal cord. This was caused from the accident he had."

"Will they be able to correct it?"

"Well, they are going to try."

While my father was in the Davenport, Iowa State Hospital for two years, Mother made arrangements to take the children to visit him only once. It was so far away, we couldn't make the trip to see him very often. We had to get someone with an automobile to take us to Davenport, and that cost money that we just didn't have.

Arrangements were made to visit Dad in Davenport. We all went and we were taken on a tour through the hospital. It was a fascinating experience for us. They had a large room with every part of the human body on display. The skulls lined up on shelves and the skeletons in rows made a gruesome sight. However, the cadavers that still grew hair and nails were so grotesque that it left an indelible impression on our minds. This array of horrors would leave any child with a chilling memory, but especially for young Amish children, who normally lead such sheltered lives, this experience was unforgettable.

Lancaster, Pennsylvania

Uncle Judas's Influence

A father with seven children under twelve years plus a wife with a newborn has a lot of responsibility. However, our father had been admitted to the hospital and all his responsibility now fell onto our mother. She had her hands doubly full with the farm, children, and her own duties.

Mom would get up at 4:30 A.M. to build a fire in the old iron cooking stove. Then she would get the boys up to get the cows ready for milking. While the boys got the cows ready and did the other chores, she placed the iron skillet on the stove, and sliced and placed the cooked cornmeal in the pan to fry while she went to the barn to milk a cow by hand. After one cow was done, she ran to the house to turn her mush over to fry the opposite side and called the girls to get up. Then she went back to milk another cow. The boys continued their milking until all the cows were done.

The milk was carried to the house to be separated. A separator is a machine that separates the cream from the milk. The cream would run into a five-gallon can to be shipped away. A milk truck would pick it up. The milk would run into a five-gallon bucket and then be carried to the pigs. A dish for the dog and cats would be filled as well. While the milk was being separated, the smaller children would get an empty glass and run to fill it with warm, fresh milk and drink it.

After all the chores were done, we had breakfast at 7:15 A.M. On school days we left the house at 8:00 A.M. In the evening the younger children helped to milk in Mom's place.

However, our daily duties weren't Mother's only problems. She received a letter from state authorities saying that they wanted to see her concerning Father's expenses and who was to take care of them.

Mom and Dad didn't have any insurance because the Amish people did not believe in having insurance with insurance companies, as most people do today. The Amish believe in taking care of their own.

Mom learned that she had a bigger problem yet. She and Dad didn't have a will made. Since there was no will made out, it was necessary to appoint a guardian to take care of Dad's money. Mom couldn't use his money for the family. The family was to stay on the farm. That was in our favor. The state agreed to take care of part of the expenses, and the Amish congregation picked up the remainder.

Mom's brother, Uncle Judas, was a tall man with dark eyes and hair, who lived one mile across the field. He tried to help her make decisions in respect to her husband's finances. Eventually she gave this responsibility entirely to him. In retrospect, I still don't understand why my uncle did the things he did in his role as family advisor. When the money was turned over to him, he not only took Father's share, he took Mother's also. He told Mom he would get our groceries as we needed them.

Father had had the outbuildings remodeled and painted before we moved to the farm. Father's dream was to do the house at a later date. But he was hospitalized before he was able to complete this.

The first year that Father was hospitalized, the Amish community helped Mom and the boys farm. After the first year, it began to be old hat and help came more and more seldom. However, Mom and the boys continued the farming on their own.

My oldest brother, William, was in fourth grade when Mother took him out of school to help her on the farm. The second boy was Levi, and he went through the fifth grade before Mom took him out to help William. They had to grow up fast and work extra hard for young boys their age.

When Uncle Judas was appointed Father's guardian, he volunteered to take Mom's share of the money along with Dad's. When we needed groceries, Uncle Judas took it upon himself to buy flour, sugar, yeast, Karo syrup, baking powder, soda, salt, oatmeal, and cornmeal. Anything else we had to raise and cold pack and then store away for the winter season. Sometimes his calculations were off and we ended up with too much or too little of important staples.

One family in Indiana heard of our plight and offered to help. They wrote to the Amish newspaper The Budget, printed in Sugarcreek, Ohio. It circulated among the Amish communities in the country. They started a money shower, asking people to send some money to help the family.

However, Uncle Judas saw this plea for help in the paper. He began coming over to the house every day when it was time for the mailman. He even had the nerve to meet the mailman at his mailbox and asked him if he wouldn't leave my mother's mail at his box. The mailman, of course, refused.

Uncle Judas came over regularly to check with Mother to see if she received any money from the shower. One day for instance, she had received three letters. He asked her for them. She turned them over to him like a little girl obeying her father. My mother didn't say much at first. However, when she needed money and Uncle Judas refused, then she really was upset and complained. She told us children what he was doing. She was upset because she couldn't even get Jell-O or a box of tapioca for a special dish once in a while. She couldn't understand what the shower money had to do with Dad's money. Why was Uncle Judas doing this to us?

Uncle Judas carefully confiscated all the envelopes that contained money for the family. Mother didn't get one cent from that shower! She never did know how much was sent to her or where it came from.

In the spring of that year, some cows and heifers had calves. One calf grew up to be a grade-A bull. Uncle Judas offered Mother twenty-five dollars for the bull. This upset Mother because she knew he was worth more than that. Another farmer had offered her eighty-five dollars. She told Uncle Judas she wasn't interested in selling it.

Mother had to buy eye blinders for the bull, because he was dangerous. When we were told to go after the cows, we were afraid of him. He would charge us girls if we weren't careful. We always tried to sneak up behind the herd and get the cows moving before he spotted us. Sometimes he would lift his head up to try to look under his

41

blinders to see who or what was coming toward him. Then we would run with everything that was in us.

The bull was such a danger to us that Mother decided to sell him for the best offer. Two weeks after she sold him, Uncle Judas found out about it. He came over and asked Mother for the money from the sale of the bull.

"I don't have any money," she told him.

"What did you do with it?"

"I can take care of my own business."

He couldn't understand what she did with it and left. Mother wasn't the kind of woman that would argue. However, she had decided it just wasn't any of his business.

What my mother wanted to do was finish Father's dream. It was always Father's dream to have a porch built onto the southeast end of the house. When Mother decided she was going to complete his dream, she ran into trouble. She still blames our Uncle Judas.

Following the sale of the bull, my mother went to Independence and deposited the money from the sale in a bank, even though it was against the Amish tradition. Our Amish community didn't believe that you should collect interest on money, because you didn't earn it from labor. But in our case, this was a last resort, since Mother was determined to keep the family together and complete Father's dream. We lived by the axiom, "Where there is a will, there is a way." Mother had the will to keep the family together, and she decided to do it any way she could.

The Amish in our settlement were only allowed to earn up to as much money as would not obligate them to pay federal income taxes. Now that Mother had deposited the money in the bank, she would not have it readily available to give to her brother in case he should ask for it, and she didn't have to lie about it either. This was the easiest way, since he was constantly overstepping the boundaries of his authority.

Mother ordered the porch materials from a lumberyard in Independence. She said she would pay for it when she picked it up. The day she was supposed to pick up the material, she couldn't get to town. She asked her modern friend from Littleton if she would pick it up for her. Her friend said she would be more than happy to pick it up.

Mother paid for the material on her next trip to Independence. Soon after, Mother realized she had forgotten to order the entrance door. She asked her friend if she would order the door for her when she went to town. A few days later, the lady stopped over and said the man at the lumber-yard claimed they were not allowed to extend credit to Katie Troyer.

Mother's friend asked her, "When you went to town, you paid for the other material, didn't you?"

"Yes, I did."

It was then that Mother realized her brother had probably said something. She needed the door, so she hitched up the horse and buggy and drove into Independence to get the door and pay for it. When she arrived home, she stated, "Judas probably couldn't figure out how I was able to get the material. Well, where there is a will there is a way."

Mother and the two eldest brothers were planning to add the porch themselves. An Amish man asked her, "What are you going to build with your lumber?"

"I want to tear down the unsafe open porch and build a new enclosed one."

"Who's going to build it?"

"I thought the boys could help me."

"Well, you know it's our tradition to help each other with something like that."

"I don't want to be a burden to anyone."

"When did you plan on building it?"

"Next week."

"I'll have all the men come over Tuesday afternoon. It's a small job and we can have it done in half a day."

"I'll have dinner for you then."

"No, that won't be necessary."

After the neighbor man left, Mother was upset. She said, "It may be their tradition to help each other with something like this, but it is also my duty to serve them a meal in return." Then she did a little more thinking.

My brother William finally commented,"Maybe they don't want to eat here since Dad's not here."

Mother agreed."They don't want to take food away from the table, so I have more for my children," she added.

Mother never did completely accept the neighbor's refusal and regarded it as a personal affront, not being allowed to furnish their dinner. However, she accepted it because they insisted on having it that way.

Mother was well pleased with the porch when it was completed. She placed her treadle sewing machine on the porch to do her sewing for the winter. We children enjoyed the new porch as much as she did.

On a cold autumn Sunday, the brothers did their chores and came in for breakfast. After breakfast they raised to their feet and picked up their harmonicas. They started playing the harmonicas on their way upstairs to get ready for church. With the sound of music, the girls' feet started tapping while they rushed around to wash the dishes and get ready for church.

When everybody was ready to leave, one of the brothers said, "Alma has no shoes on." Mother replied "Yes, I know. She doesn't have any. She has none to wear."

After church on our way home we stopped to see Uncle Judas at his home. Uncle walked to the buggy and mother said,"We need some money."

Uncle Judas asked, "What do you need it for?"

Mother took her hand and pulled the covers off my feet. "This girl needs shoes," she said.

His eyes opened wide with surprise and he answered, "Yes, she needs shoes. We'll have to see to it that she gets shoes." Mother covered my cold red feet up again and we left for home.

The following week mother asked me to put my feet on a piece of paper. She used a pencil to outline my feet to get my size for a pair of shoes.

The Farm

Last night I had a dream that I was back on the farm again. In my dream I was instantly that little five-year-old Amish girl with blonde hair and blue eyes, living on a farm in Iowa. Scenes of my childhood came vividly to my eyes.

When I actually was five years old, I remember I used to step outside the house and see the wind spinning the wheel on top of the windmill. The mill was my biggest temptation on the farm; I knew it was a no-no. One day as I watched the wheel rolling, I walked down the hill to the old gray steel-framed mill. I started to climb the windmill feeling guilty and knowing Mother always told us children to stay off it. We might fall and get hurt, she always cautioned. When I came to the top, I clung to the steel frame and looked out into the sky. I watched a bird flying alone and wished I could fly like a bird or a plane. I admired the height of the beautiful clear blue sky. It looked so peaceful.

I stood on top of the mill, looking out over the old homestead. I could see the hand water pump standing underneath the old gray windmill. I could see the flowers in full bloom in the garden. I could see the rows of vegetables outline, with a row of rhubarb and horseradish. On the opposite side grew a row of fruit trees and a grape arbor. We children had to help hoe the garden, pick vegetables, and clean them for cold-packing for the cold winter season that was only a couple of months away.

The old two-story house we lived in sat on a hill above the old mill. The house was painted white and had a stone foundation that rose to about three feet up from the ground on the west side. On the south side of the house was a cement slab leading to the screened porch, where Mother stored her washer when it was not in use. Every Monday she would pull the old clothes washer out on the slab to do the laundry. At that time, we had a washer with a hand agitator and wringer.

45

When I was about seven years old, Mother managed to get an automatic agitator and wringer, powered by a noisy gasoline engine. The clothes were rinsed twice and then hung on the clothesline to dry. Doing the laundry for nine people was an all-day job.

The three solid irons were placed on the wood stove to heat. The clothes were ironed as they were brought in from the line. Two irons were put on to heat while the other was being used. It was a continuous walk back and forth to the stove and ironing board until all the clothes were finished.

A young willow tree about the size of a dogwood grew in the southeast side of the yard. Little did we know at the time we moved here that it would be our discipline tree. It didn't take long to find out that when you didn't obey, a soft branch was broken off and cleaned for our discipline. Mother spoke once and we knew we had better listen or else. Sometimes she would order one of us to go and fetch her a switch. With no hesitation, we ran out to get her a willow branch. Whenever Mother had the willow branch lying beside her or in her hand, we knew she wouldn't hesitate to use it with a swish over our little bottoms and legs. It only took one or two strikes to get us in order. The willow branch did the talking for her. It did the job very well. Burn? Wow-wee! We would jump!

Looking down from the windmill, I could see the path leading to the old hand pump where we fetched our buckets of water for household use. We had to carry two buckets in the morning and four in the evening. This doesn't include how many it took on washdays, which was enough for the washer and two rinse tubs. It was easier to carry a bucket in each hand rather than just one. One made you lopsided! It felt better to have both shoulders dragged to the ground. I wonder if this is where I got my long arms?

There weren't any drains in the house. The used water would be poured in five-gallon buckets for slop. The slop was carried from the house down to the pigpen for the hogs to drink. The pigpen was located about five feet to the north side of the windmill, and the chickenhouse was on the south side of the water pump. It was the children's responsibility

46

to feed and water the chickens and gather the eggs twice a day. How we hated to take care of chickens.

Seldom could I walk in the hen house in my bare feet without getting my feet dirty. I never wore shoes in the summer. When I went to gather eggs, I would peer inside to determine whether I could avoid the chicken manure on the floor. On tiptoes I would step in gingerly, but to no avail. "Oh no, not again!" I'd shout. The goo would ooze up between my toes. As I would gather the eggs, I would come upon a biddy that didn't want to be disturbed from sitting on her nest of eggs. When I reached to get the eggs under her, she would peck me with her beak. I would jump with fright and then go back again for the eggs. Some hens pecked much harder than others. You never knew what to expect.

On Saturdays, we children would get the garden hoe to clean the roosting shelves. The chicken droppings were spread evenly on the garden for fertilizer.

There were days when our work was done and the chickens served a different purpose. I would go in the hen house and catch a beautiful banty rooster to pick the prettiest feather that he had. My sister and brother would do the same. The things we did next really stretched the imagination. We pretended these feathers were our horses. Whoever had the prettiest feathers had the best team of horses. We would pretend we were working in the fields or going to see some friends or to town.

Built adjacent to the chicken house was our outhouse. If that little wooden building could have talked, what stories it would tell. I remember scrubbing it out on Saturdays. We used the Sears Roebuck catalogue instead of toilet paper. When I saw the catalogue, I couldn't help but think of a lonely widowed Amish man who lived in our community. He longed so for a wife. One day he saw a woman in the Sears catalogue and placed an order. How astonished he was to receive a dress. "I didn't want the dress; I wanted what was in it," he grumbled. It's a shame that he was so naive.

There was a winding creek running though the barnyard behind the outbuildings, down past the garden, across the boundary line, and through the neighbors' woods. This

47

had several deep holes, where we would pull our ankle-length dresses up over our knees to go wading. This we would do at every opportunity, enjoying the cool water on hot summer days.

Grandpa and Grandma from Oklahoma would visit us for the summer season. When they caught us in the creek, Grandpa would yell at us,"Get out of there and let your dresses down; your legs are showing!"

We weren't the only ones that enjoyed the creek. The ducks enjoyed the water also. The cows and horses would drink from the creek, and I can't forget the watchdogs. They enjoyed getting in the creek to bathe and cool down on hot days. As they climbed out on the bank, they would shake their whole bodies and get us all wet. With a new dog who wasn't sure about the water, we would throw him in, and before long he was enjoying himself with the rest of the barnyard family.

On the path between the house and the barn we had a natural sandbox, large enough for the younger children to enjoy playing in. Using our foot for a pattern, we would add water to pack the sand, and upon removing the foot, we would have an entrance to the tunnel.

On the southwest side of the creek and barnyard was a tillable field. This field was usually underwater during the spring floods. High water would take the good soil with it and leave the field covered with sand. Where there was sand, there were sandburrs.

Early one evening, Elizabeth and I were asked to go after the cows. We ran down and through the barnyard, raising our dresses to cross the creek. "Let's take a short cut through the field," I said. Elizabeth agreed as she ran along beside me. About twenty feet into the field, she hollered,"Ouch!" I hollered back "Ouch! Ouch!" There we stopped. We both lamented,"This hurts. Oh! Nah, there's no place to step." We tried to clean our feet and give each other support while doing so. It was impossible. We started crying and screaming for help.

Grandpa, hearing us, yelled,"What's wrong?"

"Our feet are covered with sandburrs. The field is covered with them."

Grandpa came to our rescue. He carried us both out of the field, one under each arm. Then he told us to take the pasture path, which we usually did. We didn't disagree.

My brother Daniel came along while I was surveying the homestead from the windmill and caught me.

"What are you doing up there?" asked Daniel.

"I wish I could fly."

"You'd better get down before Mom sees you."

"All right, but I'm closer to heaven up here." I climbed back down.

"If Mom catches you, you're in trouble."

When I reached the ground, I said, "It's really nice up there."

"Let me go up quickly," he whispered.

"All right."

Daniel was climbing up the old windmill when Mother walked outside from the house and caught him. Guess who was in trouble?

Kalona, Iowa

Planting and Harvesting

There was only one Amish sect or denomination in Buchanan County, Iowa. However, in some areas there are many. There are as many as twelve denominations of Amish in Holmes County, Ohio. As an example of types, there are two different denominations of horse-and-buggy Amish. One is named the Behinders, and the other is called the Old Order Amish. Our Buchanan County denomination fell somewhere between the Behinders and the Old Order Amish.

The Behinders are the Schwartzentrubers. Their belief in living more naturally is even stronger than the Old Order Amish. They don't believe in putting gravel on their driveways. Their income is to the limit so they don't have to pay income tax. They don't believe in having anything to do with the government. Their dress code is dark for the men and women. They have their own school. They have their own insurance. If one has a fire they all get together and pay for it, and with their hard working hands, build it up again.

One of the more modern sects is the Beachy Amish. They use a black automobile for transportation. The women's and men's style of dress is different from the traditional Amish style, yet an outsider can't tell that there is a difference. Amishmen probably all look alike to the outsider's eye because the clothing styles are so similar from sect to sect.

The Beachy have many more modern conveniences in their homes, such as electricity, telephones, wall-to-wall carpeting, drapes, and other modern appliances. However, the Old Order Amish use gasoline-powered washers, solid irons, and horses to do their farming and harvesting. Water is drawn from the well by windmill or gas engine. For light, the Old Order use kerosene lamps and gasoline lanterns.

We had a team of draft horses that we used for farming. The boys would hitch the team to a plow to till the ground. It was a continuous back-and-forth pattern, since the plow

51

tilled over one row of ground at a time and had a seat for one driver. Every so often, my brother would stop and let the horses rest.

Midmorning and midafternoon, Mom would ask one of us younger ones to carry a jug of water out to the field for our brother. Sometimes we would surprise him with spearmint tea.

It took a whole day for one of my brothers to till an entire field. Although the Amish are allowed to own a pocket watch, wristwatches are not permissible. My brothers didn't have a pocket watch to tell when it was dinnertime, so, like the Indians, they went by the sun. Judging by the sun, they knew when it was 11:30 A.M. Then they would come in for dinner.

When the plowing was done, they would disc the field. With the driver standing on the rake, a team of horses pulled a large rake across the field to even up the dirt. Finally, the seeds were planted, with a prayer for a good crop according to God's will.

Once, when my brother Daniel was quite small, he lost his balance and fell, with the rake being pulled over his legs. Luckily he was all right. However, this incident scared him enough to be more careful afterward.

We had a field that had a good-sized hill. When Dad was hospitalized, Uncle Judas told Mom to farm the dangerous field. Brother William harnessed the team of working horses and hitched them to the one-row plow with a one-man seat. William went out to till the field with Mom and Brother Levi following him on foot. William started out with the reins in his hands, sitting in the seat, and at the age of thirteen had to do a man's job. Mom and Levi stood at the end of the field to watch William to make sure he was all right. He started down to till the first row. His plow promptly turned over. He quickly jumped to safety, losing his straw hat. He picked up his hat and placed it back on his head, covering his blond hair. Mother and Levi ran over to help him set the plow back up on its two wheels. William made one trip down and back. He turned around and started another row. His plow turned over the second time. Mother feared for his safety. She was angry because she had tried to tell Uncle Judas that it would be better to turn this field into a pasture for livestock. However, as the boys became older, they could see we needed more corn and hay for the animals. With Mom's consent, they decided to fence in twenty acres of the pasture at the far northwest end of the other flat fields. The dangerous field was converted to a pasture. There was a piece of ground that was not fenced and was used for pasture alone. Uncle Judas always said,"It is no good."

The brothers knew we needed more feed for the animals. Against Uncle Judas's wishes, Mom, William, and Levi loaded the barbed wire, fence posts, post digger, and tools on the hay wagon and headed out to fence in the ground that Uncle Judas always said was no good. They added a field to the third one on the northwest side that couldn't be seen from the house. The field was plowed, disced, and raked, and corn was planted. We hoped the earth was fertile. When it was time to harvest the corn, we had to build an extra corncrib, because the new field brought such an excellent yield of corn.

My brothers were proud of God for making it possible. Despite the negative leadership Uncle Judas had given us, my brothers showed us all that what Mom preached to us was true:"Where there is a will, there is a way."

Our fields were fertilized with natural fertilizer from the barn. When the barn was cleaned out, the manure was spread over the fields. Uncle Judas wouldn't let Mom fertilize the fields except in this way.

We would rotate the crops every year. Mom knew what to plant in each field every year, and she taught the boys what to plant. For example, where there were oats one year, she would plant hay the following year. After hay, she would plant corn and then wheat. She would never plant the same kind of crop twice. She planted peanuts in the sandburrs. When we needed molasses, she would plant sugarcane to make sorghum.

The Amish believe everything should be done manually. When it was time to make hay, the hay was mowed and laid out for a day or two to dry. Then it was raked into a row and laid for a half-day to make sure it wasn't green or wet.

When it was time to bring the hay to the barn, everybody gave a hand. We would hitch working horses to the hay wagon, and we younger children took turns driving the team in the fields. When it was my turn to drive, we hitched the hay loader to the end of the wagon and I had to keep a horse on each side of the row. Two of my brothers, each with a hay fork, were on the wagon. The hay loader picked up the loose hay and dropped it on the wagon. They would take the fork and stack the hay evenly. The hay piled up until it finally covered above the ladder where the driver stood. Since this was the first time for me to drive, my attention was on the horses, to make sure they stayed in a row. I ignored what was happening in the wagon behind me. Suddenly I felt the hay moving up my back. I looked around and Brother Levi smiled, noticing I was frightened. He assured me,"You'll be all right; just climb the wagon ladder, and when we go higher, you stay behind the ladder until we are loaded. The ladder will keep you from falling off."

"Okay," I said.

When the wagon was loaded, my brothers called out,"Whoa!" I stopped the horses and looked up. Then I was really scared. I couldn't see my brothers for the mountain of hay above my head. Soon I felt them moving to the front and they asked,"Want to come up here?"

I didn't know what I wanted at the time, but I answered,"How?"

Levi leaned down and reached out his arm and said,"Give me your right hand and I'll pull you up."

"All right." I reached up and he grabbed my hand and pulled me up to the very top. My stomach felt strange. "Oh, we're so high, won't we tip?" I asked.

"Nah, just sit down in the middle. I'll drive the horses in." I gave him the reins, and he walked the horses to the barn.

The wagon was parked on the east end outside of the barn to unload the hay. We had a four-tooth fork connected to a rope that ran on a pulley up to the haymow. Then the rope ran out and tied to a horse in the driveway. My two brothers would be in the haymow and one on the hay wagon to load the fork. When it was ready, they would yell at me, "Ready!" I would drive the horse on foot out away from the barn, pulling the load up into the loft. When it arrived in the mow where they wanted it, one of my brothers would yell, "Whoa!"

The brother in the barn would pull on the rope to the fork to release the hay when I stopped the horse. We would repeat this process until the hay was unloaded.

Sometimes we would borrow a neighbor's hay wagon so when one was unloading, the other one was being loaded. Mom would take care of the fork outside the wagon and send one brother up into the haymow. The other two were sent back to the field.

I remember I thought I was really a big girl out there helping my big brothers. I felt I had to act like I was really brave, although inside I was really scared. After a while I became used to it and the job didn't bother me anymore and I enjoyed it.

When it was time to do the wheat, it was combined and shocked. Then all the neighbors got together and helped each other. Every farmer took turns getting the wheat in. We called this "threshing season." The farmer's wife was informed when she was going to have the men, and she would prepare dinner on the day they worked on her farm.

After everybody's wheat was in, we all gathered together and had an ice cream supper. Every family would take a full freezer of ice cream along, so there was a variety of ice cream. It was a way of showing appreciation to the others and a way to get some relaxation after a month of hard work.

In autumn the corn was picked. Mom and my older brother would put a corn picking glove on and use the box-grain wagon to throw the corn in. The corn was picked and husked by hand. When the wagon was loaded, it was shoveled into the corncrib. This cycle was repeated until all the corn was harvested. When we needed corn for the animals, we had to shell the corn off the cob. We had a corn sheller sitting at the end of the crib. We younger children would shell daily as we needed it. One would feed the machine as the other one would turn the crank.

We pretended it was something wild and hungry. The faster we turned the crank, the angrier the monster would get, until it would eat the corn off in a matter of seconds. The monster would spill the corn into a container and spit the cob out the end. We used the cobs to start the fire in our wood and coal stove.

We would harvest the vegetables and fruit. We had green beans, peas, tomatoes, carrots, red and white radishes, red beets, and corn. We would use field corn when it was new; we had to get it before it hardened. It really was good. I hated green peas. We planted an area of potatoes. Everybody would help with this, because it was a big job. The brothers would get the field ready. Then with a team of horses they would use a plow to make the row. We dropped the eye potatoes in a row a foot apart and covered them up. In the fall, my brothers used the plow again to dig them up. We would all go out and pick the potatoes up. They were stored in the ground basement in a bin for the winter. Everybody enjoyed the potatoes on the table. We cold packed the rhubarb, plums, and apple sauce. This was our fruit on the farm. The grapes were eaten off the arbor. The arbor wasn't very big. Apples that weren't made into apple sauce or pies were wrapped individually and stored in an old milk can in the basement. In January, we would open the can and the apples were just as fresh as the day we picked them. We cold-packed the rhubarb. We ate rhubarb until I learned to hate it. Plums were the same way. I always preferred cooked cornmeal with gravy over it to any of the two fruits. We had a few strawberries. Mother would cold-pack them, too. This ruined them, or maybe I just got tired of them, too. I used to eat strawberries in our cold bread soup for supper. In the summertime, we would break a loaf of bread into bite-size pieces in a big bowl. Next we added one cup of sugar, poured cold milk over it, and mixed it. We placed the big bowl in the center of the table. A bowl of fruit was set on the table, too. Then you dipped a dipperful of bread soup in your soup bowl. Next you added one or two spoonfuls of fruit over your bread soup and ate it. We often had cornbread, milk and sugar. This was good. Brother Levi would sometimes eat leftover cornbread with milk and sugar for his breakfast cereal.

For breakfast we had pancakes with homemade syrup. Syrup consisted of 2 cups of brown sugar, 2 cups of karo syrup, 2 cups of water, and 1 teaspoon of vanilla. We brought it to a boil and boiled for ten minutes, then served it over hotcakes.

Oatmeal was our favorite cereal. However, we also had fried mush or cooked mush served with brown pan or cream of tomato gravy. Sometimes cooked mush was eaten with sugar and milk over it, like cereal. There were home fries with creamed tomato gravy for breakfast. Creamed tomato gravy was made at least once a day. For breakfast or dinner, a table without a bowl of gravy was unheard of. Sometimes we had gravy over bread. Our main meal was lunch. The meal usually consisted of potatoes, gravy, vegetable, meat, apple sauce, and a pudding or another kind of dessert.

Top: School at Berne, Indiana.
Bottom: Kalona, Iowa children walking home from school.

School Days

When we moved to Iowa, the new Amish settlement still didn't have its own school in our district. I went to Fairbank Public School for two years. With the harsh winter, the school bus couldn't make it to the house every day. My older brothers would walk to the neighbors' farm to catch the bus, but seeing me as a sickly little girl, Mother wouldn't let me walk. The snow was usually so deep it came up to the boys' knees and to my hips

"You can't go, Alma," Mother said. "You're too small." Not being able to go to school disappointed me very much.

One morning, I was almost left behind accidentally. The bus had stopped with the door closed. I was standing there waiting for the driver to open the door, but he didn't. The bus started to pull away. My eyes welled up with tears. I felt as though my eyes were ready to jump out of my head with disbelief.

I heard the children on the bus yelling. Then the bus stopped. I ran to catch it. "I'm very sorry: I didn't see you," the driver said. "Next time, knock." I thought it was strange he couldn't see me. I thought I was as big as anyone else in my class. I stepped on the bus and didn't say a word all the way to school. He had hurt my feelings. I couldn't believe he didn't see me.

At first, school was strange to me. Dutch was spoken in the home and German in the church (a little more explanation of the language spoken - not Dutch, really, but Pennsylvania German, or Deutch). School was my first real experience with the English language. It rather frightened me, and then, too, the Amish children were also set apart because of their style of clothes. I didn't really envy the other students, and I liked school.

My dress was a solid color and came down to my ankles. Over it I wore an apronlike covering. I had two school dresses for the week. Other girls wore pretty outfits, sometimes skirts and jumpers, with blouses or sweaters.

Mother always said,"Don't wish for what somebody else has, and don't be jealous."

Everybody spoke English. That was a strange and foreign language to us Amish-speaking children. The teacher was familiar with the situation, having had Amish speaking children in her classes before. The teacher and the other students work with me to help me learn English. But for a long time I would still speak Amish. At recess or as soon as school was dismissed, we Amish children would speak Amish to each other. The teacher would hear us. "You're never going to learn to speak English if you keep on speaking Dutch," she would say, reminding us to speak English. That was the hardest thing to remember when I had another Amish friend by my side. It wasn't until halfway through my first year that I began to speak English regularly. I would rather not say anything than speak English.

During my second year, the public school had pictures taken of all the students. This was against the Amish belief. When the pictures were sent home to the parents, the Amish parents decided it was best to buy them and then bury them in the ground.

Mother bought the pictures, but kept two pictures of each of us children and hid them without telling anyone.

During my third year of school, a new school opened in Littleton, Iowa, as a public school of that district. We had to furnish our own transportation. It was about two and a half miles to and from school, which we walked most of the time. Sometimes we were treated to our horse and hack buggy for our trip. A hack buggy is similar to a buckboard with no top and only one seat. The young ones would sit in the buggy box in the rear while my sister Susan sat in the front with the driver.

The horse and buggy was parked on the school grounds, under the shade trees in the south corner of the two-acre lot. One day, Brother Levi went to get the rig with Susan, Daniel, Elizabeth, and Henry Jr., and me all packed in. When we left the school grounds, they walked the rig, because the children were walking on both sides. Some students made fun of us, and others watched with interest. One kid was as ornery as the day was long. He walked up to another boy, who was walking beside us admiring the horses, and pushed him in the path of the rig's wheel. I saw it happen and screamed, "The front wheel went over that boy!"

The frightened boy jumped to his feet and ran. Before we could ask or even check to see if he was all right, he was gone. The schoolteacher heard the screams and checked to see what had happened. The culprit who did the pushing was punished. He had to stay after school for an hour for two weeks. Pushing someone in front of a buggy was a serious offense.

Even though I had missed so much school the previous year, I was happy to see that I had all S's on my report card. That was the best you could get in those days. About a month after school started in Littleton, though, I received a setback. I was doing my arithmetic when the teacher came over to me and said, "Alma, I received a report from the state concerning you. Since you missed so many days last year, they want you to take the first grade over again, even though you had passing grades."

In my shyness, I just looked up at her and nodded my head. I was disappointed. I liked what I was doing and didn't want to repeat what I had done last year. I didn't argue the case, but dropped back a year with my sister Elizabeth. Later in the year I was bored and started to work out of another book. The teacher told me that I was doing fourth-grade problems.

The Amish decided to open their own school about four miles from Littleton out in the country. They obtained a certified teacher from Oelwein, Iowa.

The school was a one-room building. There was a small shed out back where wood and coal were stored for the winter. The eighth-grade boys had to bring in some coal and wood every afternoon before they went home and bank the fire in the large pot-belly stove for the night.

There were two outhouses close by, one for the girls and one for the boys. The hitching posts for the parents to tie up their horses were on the north side along the school building.

We carried our lunches to school every day. There was no such thing as a cafeteria. When the sun was shining and it was warm outside, we would grab our lunch buckets and run outside to sit under a big shade tree. We had an hour for lunch. Usually after eating we would play. We'd play ball, jump rope, ride the merry-go-round, and swing on the swings. We didn't have modern playground equipment, but we were content with what we had. We also would swing and turn somersaults on the hitching posts. It was fun turning those somersaults, but many times we'd catch the bottom edge of our ankle-length dress on the heel of our shoes and tear out the hem. We sat through school with a torn hem and fixed it when we arrived home.

If the weather was bad, we played inside. The teacher had a handcrank record player she let us use, or we'd write on the backboard or play jacks. Our teacher wasn't just someone who was there for a paycheck. She was a teacher, friend, and mother and always had her pupils under control. She would explain, "If there isn't order when the people from the state visit our school, it can be closed."

One day you could have heard a pin drop. I looked up from my studies. I had a question and was looking around the room for the teacher. All the other students were busy on their assignments. I started to get up, but then I noticed some strange people in modern clothes in the back of the room. Oh, the people from the state, I thought.

So I raised my hand and the teacher, with a smile on her face, nodded to me. I quietly went up to her and asked her the question. I don't think very many students had heard those visitors come in. I hadn't. I was surprised to see them there. They were gone by recess time. It sure was nice that we were all working hard when they arrived. That was a good mark for the teacher. I could tell she was proud of her students.

The school had an old-fashioned hand bell to ring when it was time to start classes, reminiscent of the pioneer days. When we heard that bell, we all ran for the schoolhouse. We had just three minutes to be in our seats. The Amish country school's enrollment for the first year was fourteen, the next eighteen, and the third year twenty-three. One teacher taught all the students from the kindergarten through the eighth grade. She'd spend time with one age group, then give them an assignment, then go on to another group. Sometimes we'd split up into little circles to do our work.

When I was in first grade at Littleton, I realized how I felt about the outside world. One day when I was playing with some non-Amish girls, one of them asked, "Would you spend the night with me?"

Until this moment I had been unaware of the fact that I was afraid to visit with a "modern" family. I was fully at ease with my friend and liked her as a classmate, but I was afraid to go to her home. I didn't know what to say to her, because I didn't want to hurt her feelings. I could tell the little girl really wanted me to come home with her. Shyly, I shook my head in the negative. I told her, "I will ask my mother."

I was so afraid that I never asked. I just told the girl the next day, "I can't stay over."

I imagined her family would fight. Because all the rest of the world had just completed World War II, I thought all the people who weren't Amish were fighting all the time. The Amish are peace-loving people. They do not believe in violence. Violence was one way we knew that my father was not himself anymore. My father wasn't a violent man before his accident. We knew something was seriously wrong as time went by after his accident. His mental attitude was changing too rapidly, and this wasn't normal.

One sunny morning, we children took the buckboard to our Amish school. On our way home we saw dark clouds approaching fast. We hurried the horse, trying to beat the storm home. As we reached the drive, the wind was gusting with great force. The strong winds lifted one side of the rig, and we came in on two wheels. We all screamed with fright, shifting our weight to bring the rig back down. Daniel parked beside the east end of the barn, where the wind wasn't as strong. He was unhitching the horse when the wind slowed up. He yelled, "Run for the house!"

We three girls ran for the house, leaving Daniel behind. Susan and Elizabeth reached the house, with me right behind them. But before I had a chance to get hold of the door, a strong wind lifted me off my feet, carrying me away from the house.

My first impression was "Oh, I can fly!" which is what I always wanted to do. As I was flying away from the house, I looked back to see if my sisters saw me flying.

"Come on, Alma!" Elizabeth yelled, watching me fly.

The wind had taken my breath. I looked down and realized I wasn't flying, the wind was carrying me without touching the ground.

This frightened me. With my toes digging down in my shoes, I tried to reach the ground, but to no avail. I started to swing my feet hard under the skirt of my big dress. But that just made me go away from the house faster. I was flying into the yard when I managed to grab a hold of a tree in the yard.

Elizabeth yelled again. "Hang on, Alma!" She stood watching from the porch in fear.

I couldn't answer. I hung to the tree for dear life, hoping the wind would ease a little. When it did slow down, I ran to the house to safety.

The next day, we heard a chicken house had been turned over and a barn roof had been blown off. We realized a tornado had gone through. God was with us and knew how lucky we had been. That cured my wishing to fly like a bird or a plane.

The Stranger

That particular summer morning was turning into a beautiful sunny day, with the temperature at a pleasant eight-six degrees. My teenage brothers didn't hesitate in doing the morning chores, happily hitching the team of draft horses that they would need for the day's work. Their younger sisters also busied themselves with their routine.

Susan, age eleven, mixed the bread dough before breakfast. She added four packages of dry yeast to four and a half cups of warm water in a mixing bowl and let the yeast dissolve. Then she added six tablespoons of sugar, 1/4 cup of melted shortening, two tablespoons of salt, and seven cups of flour. She beat this mixture until smooth, then added more flour (about six cups), a little at a time. She let the dough rise and punched it down. Then Susan formed four loaves and let them rise. She baked them for about forty-five to sixty minutes at 350 degrees. The dough would rise while they had breakfast. Elizabeth fetched the water from the well in the old wooden bucket and provided an armful of wood for the kitchen stove.

As we sat at the table, Mother directed,"Daniel, bring in the buggy horse and hitch it up, because I'm going to Independence today."

"May I go with you?"

"No. I want you boys to help each other repairing the broken fence so the cows won't get out and forage in the neighbors' corn. That fence has to be repaired today for sure."

When Mother journeyed to Independence, it was an all-day trip, easily a two-hour ride each way by buggy. Mother readied herself and left early in the day. The boys loaded their tools on the hay wagon and set off to mend the fence. Susan kneaded her bread dough and covered it once again to let it rise. Then she started washing the milking equipment. While washing the separator, the girls heard an automobile pull to a stop out front. Susan and Elizabeth stopped what they were doing and looked through the window. A man was sitting in the vehicle parked out by the road.

He opened his car door, stepped out for a few moments, and just stood there surveying the house. The man appeared well tailored and affluent.

As the man started walking toward the house, Susan, the elder of the girls, said, "Elizabeth, take Annie Baby upstairs and hide under the bed. Be very quiet and don't make any noise. Mother says to always be cautious of strangers when we are by ourselves."

"What about you?" Elizabeth whispered back.

"Don't worry about me; just take Annie and go before he gets to the door."

With some concern, Susan shoved Elizabeth into the kitchen and said, "Please! Take the baby upstairs and hide right now so I won't have to worry about you. And remember, no noise! I don't want him to know you are here."

Elizabeth promised and Susan sighed with relief. "Good! Go now and shut the upstairs door, too."

Susan returned to the separator room to lock the outside door, closing the kitchen door behind her. She knew the lock was not too secure, but she locked it anyway and stood on the opposite side of the room, trembling in silence. A knock came on the door. Susan stood frozen to the spot. A second knock. Still Susan refused to break her silence, hardly daring to breathe, hoping the man would leave. The third knock came immediately, followed by a harsh voice.

"Open up; I know you are in there!"

Now there was a loud banging on the door.

"Come on, open up or I'll bust it down."

Susan moved behind the door and asked timidly, "What do you want?"

She braced her foot against the locked door to help prevent it from breaking. The man shoved on the door until the lock let loose with a loud bang. Susan couldn't hold the door closed any longer. She started to cry as the man roughly pushed her back against the wall.

The man asked her if anyone else was in the house.

"No, I'm all alone."

Little did Susan know that her sisters, in their concern for her, were not hiding upstairs as they were told, but were in fact lying on the kitchen floor peering under the door to see if Susan was in any danger.

The man walked up to her and said, "I just want to talk to you." He grabbed her dress and said, "I won't hurt you."

"Please leave me alone," Susan pleaded.

With a cruel laugh, he ripped her dress down over her shoulders. "I just want to talk to you. You are a pretty little thing."

He moved closer to her as if he wanted to kiss her.

Susan struggled with him. She was afraid of him because he was stronger than she was. Fighting him off, she shouted, "I will yell for my brothers if you don't leave me alone."

"How many brothers do you have, honey?"

"I have four brothers. All I have to do is yell, and they will come running."

"Where are your brothers?"

"They are working in the barn."

"I just want to talk to you." He moved toward her once more.

"I will yell if you don't leave and leave now. My brothers can take you with no problem."

"You sure about that?"

"Yes! They are strong," she warned him, facing him eye to eye.

He backed off. Susan pulled her dress back over her shoulder, trying to gather herself together again. He looked through the window, paled, and hurriedly exited though the door. Susan walked to the window to make sure the man was really leaving and noticed the boys coming in from fixing the fence. She cried with relief and was still crying when the boys came in to see what the car was doing there.

She tried to wipe her tears away, but her brother Levi knew when he saw her that something wasn't right.

"What's wrong?"

She was crying so hard she couldn't answer.

"What happened?"

Elizabeth and Annie opened the door and excitedly started to tell him what had happened. Susan managed to get herself together and told him the story. The brothers were angry and questioned, "What can we do to prevent this from happening again?"

William and Levi continued about their duties around the farm. For the rest of the day the boys stayed close to the house. The evening chores were done early. At the dinner table, Levi announced, "William and I are going to see a friend. We know he had some puppies, and we'll see if we can still get one. We are going to raise it to be a watchdog so what happened today won't ever happen again."

Two hours later they came home with a cute collie puppy. Just like the brothers had said, we trained him to be a watchdog. And an excellent watchdog he was!

Junior: All Boy!

The first boy born after me carries our father's name. He resembled his father, too. He is two and a half years younger than me and was the first sibling I remembered growing up.

There was also Elizabeth, evenly spaced between him and me. Our ages were so close that I didn't regard her so much as a sister, but as a playmate and friend.

Junior grew up to be all boy, as they say, full of orneriness. He had the ability to make us laugh and was quite a daredevil and yet quite ambitious.

It seemed this boy was always cutting up, especially around mealtime. Mother would warn him, "Junior, you'd better watch yourself or I'll show you something."

"What will you show me?"

Junior was always ready with a smart and usually funny comeback while keeping a straight and serious innocent look on that oval, fair-complexioned face with brown eyes. The rest of us either broke out laughing or, if we were eating, forced ourselves to stifle our laughter, nearly choking on our food. Even Mother's stern facade broke many times. She had to turn herself around so Junior wouldn't see her laughing.

One beautiful Sunday, our church services were being held at the neighbors' house across the river. We had taken our horse and buggy across the woods and river for a shortcut.

When we were ready to leave, Mother asked, "Daniel, where are the boys?"

"They walked with the other boys to the woods."

"Get in the buggy; we'll pick them up on our way."

They both sat in the buggy, and we followed our morning path back to the woods, where the boys were watching something.

We stopped and asked, "What are you looking at?"

William walked over and said softly, "There is a beehive in the tree."

After we had stopped and were focusing our attention on the boys, Junior had climbed out and walked around on his own adventure.

Daniel yelled, "Junior is walking toward the swarming bee nest."

"Oh *nah!*" Mother jumped out of the buggy and ran for him.

William ordered, "Stay here! I'll get him."

He ran over and picked Junior up, fighting off the bees. Mother ordered us to get the rig moving away from the trees. She received a couple of stings. William received a couple of stings as well, and Junior, age four, was stung several times. When we arrived on the other side of the river, he became sick to his stomach. He was very ill for the rest of the evening. Mother stayed by his side throughout the night.

One spring evening, he couldn't have been more than three years old, Junior wandered out to the barn, where the older two boys were hauling horse manure. The older boys had been spreading it in the fields in preparation for the next day's plowing.

That evening, Levi had parked the spreader in the barnyard alongside the other pieces of farm machinery. Junior tried to get out of the way, but he fell and one of the heavy steel wheels ran over him. Apparently Levi hadn't seen him. It was evening, with very little light, and Amish children wear dark-colored clothing. The child started to cry, a cry of pain. The oldest brother, who had been directing the parking, ran around the back. The other brother stopped the team of horses, jumped off the spreader, and ran back to see what was wrong.

Mother could hear the child's cry from the house. She stepped outside and yelled toward the barnyard. "What's wrong?"

70

William shouted in reply,"We backed the manure spreader over Junior."

William picked Junior up and carried him to the house.

"Did you smash him?"

We girls were in the kitchen helping to prepare supper. We froze when we heard the question and almost dropped the plates. What horrors flashed through our minds. We were relieved when we heard William holler,"No! It just went over his legs."

"Are his legs okay?"

"He's all right; that crying he did was more of fright than pain."

Mother examined his legs under the kitchen kerosene lantern. "Boy! Are we lucky."

We girls rushed over to check, too. Susan scooped Junior into her arms and carried him to the living room, where he received a lot of attention that night. That wasn't the first or last time Junior had wandered on the farm and was injured.

When he was four, Junior had gone after the cows with his older brother. William opened the barn door to let the cows in for milking and asked Junior to chase them into the barn. The entrance was about two feet higher than the ground, and the cows had to jump to get through.

My little brother thought he could do what his big brothers could. He was full of ambition and daring. However, he didn't realize the dangers around animals. He was following the cows too closely, and when the last cow came in, he grabbed her ankle and barked like a dog. This surprised the cow, and she jumped and her hind foot came back and hit him in the forehead. He was knock down and out.

When William locked the cows in their stall, he went to the door to close it. He found Junior lying on the ground. He had to look twice to make sure he was seeing right. He bent down and Junior started to cry. William noticed Junior had a gash and was bleeding from the forehead. He picked him up and carried him to the house. Of course, Mother and Junior's sisters took care of him for the rest of the evening.

71

Mother commanded,"Don't let him go to sleep for the first several hours." We girls were surprised with her statement. We asked,"Why?"

Mother answered,"The doctor had told me if at any time anyone gets hit in the head, never let them go into a sound sleep. They may never wake up. So make sure you don't let him go to sleep for the first four hours."

Junior was awakened every two hours throughout the night. This was to make sure he was all right. As of today, he is still wearing the scar, although he outgrew a lot of it.

By the time Junior was seven, he was riding our buggy horse quite a bit. But he wasn't content to keep the horse's four legs on the ground. He would go out behind the barn where he couldn't be seen from the house, and then he would rear the horse up on its hind legs. He would spend a whole afternoon teaching his horse fancy tricks. But before doing so, he would always say,"Don't tell Mom I'm going out behind the barn with the horse."

Several times Junior came to his sisters, saying "Promise not to tell Mom if I tell you something."

"*Ja.*"

"The horse reared so high he went all the way over."

"Were you on the horse?"

"Yeah," he said with a daring smile.

"Did you hurt yourself?"

"Nah," He laughed impishly.

We sisters shook our heads unbelievingly. We both agreed, "One of these days you are going to get hurt." "He isn't afraid of anything," I stated. Elizabeth agreed."That's for sure." "Don't tell Mom" became a common phrase around the house when we did something we knew we weren't supposed to.

Many times when this boy was supposed to get the cows we would find him out back of the barn. Oh, how he loved that horse. He had been attracted to the fields early. Perhaps it was his love for horses and watching them work.

As ornery as he was, he decided to play a trick on Annie, who was two years younger than himself."Annie, there is a rabbit hole out in the field. Want to go see it?"

"Yeah."

"Come on, I'll show you."

Both went trotting out to the field, taking the dog along. When they reached the hole, Junior told Annie, "Where there is an entrance there is an exit, too. You stay here and watch while I go over there to see if I can't find the exit."

"All right." she replied, not knowing any better.

Junior got his dog to start digging for him while Annie stood watch over the hole. The dog dug until he hit the underground rabbit trail and then started barking.

"Can you see a rabbit?"

Annie looked down into the hole and answered, "No! I don't see one."

"Well, you have to get down closer to see."

The dog was still digging away. As she stooped down to look, a rabbit came tearing out right into Annie's face. She jumped with a scream and fell to the ground in terror. Junior burst out laughing.

"Oh! Du dummel ding du." (You dumb thing you.)

She realized the joke was on her and started laughing along with him.

Amish boy from Berne, Indiana.

Stories at the Dinner Table

Our dinner table was covered with a plain white oilcloth. The place settings consisted of a variety of dishes. A water glass was placed by each setting.

Water glasses were filled with water from a pitcher before anyone was seated. The food was served in large bowls, and when the food was passed, everyone was to place the amount that they could eat on their plate. Each plate was to be empty when one finished eating. There is no waste allowed in an Amish home. Leftover food was placed in smaller containers and kept in an icebox. This food was always used later in some way.

For good table manners, children were taught at a young age that you chew with your mouth closed and you don't talk with your mouth full.

Only in summer did we have an iceman. He delivered ice twice a week to the Amish homes. On hot summer days we would serve spearmint tea instead of water. The spearmint grew wild on the farm. Spearmint tea was a treat for us, just like soft drinks are for today's families.

When everyone was gathered at the dinner table, the conversation would lead to storytelling. Mother would tell us about the Oklahoma farm. She and Dad had a farm in Maize County. That's where I was born, at home, in 1940.

Mom would start the story by saying, "Your father was one of the best farmers in the area. He lived on his father's farm. They operated the farm while his aging parents lived in the grandfather's house."

This practice is common among the Amish as the parents get up in years. Although the children take over the main work of the farm, the older folks still help out. "We had eleven hired hands on the three-hundred-acre farm. Your father worked it in the traditional Amish way. We didn't have any modern conveniences, so he used horses instead of tractors. I always saw to it that the hired help were fed their breakfast and dinner."

"You cooked for all those men?" I asked.

"*Ja*, everyday. Three times a day. We had nine white fellows, one Indian, and one black. On the first day that the black man came to work, I noticed that he wasn't getting ready for breakfast with the others.

"I asked, 'Where is the new man at?'

'Don't know,' was the reply.

"I went out to look for him and found him on the porch. 'Why aren't you inside getting ready to eat?' I asked. He told me he didn't know if he should come inside because he was black.

"'What?' I said. 'When you work for us, you eat with everybody else. In our house, regardless of what color you are, nobody is any better than the other.'

"I led him into the kitchen and told the other hired men that the black man worked here just like they did and he ate there at the table, too. Just like they did. Everyone agreed with me. And you know what?"

"No! What?" I questioned.

"He turned out to be one of our best workers, too."

"Really?"

"Yeah. Your father needed all the help he could get on the farm, because he baled hay and sold it. The hay was shipped to other states, and he had a deadline to meet. That was hard to do sometimes.

"We had a large number of hogs, but one year they contracted a disease known as black feet and we lost them."

"What's black feet, Mom?" Daniel asked.

"Black feet is a fatal poison, and when you cut a dead animal open, it had black under the skin.

76

"Black feet disease is caused by a bacteria called clostridium noryi. It produces a fatal toxin or poison. Noryi also causes gas gangrene infections in humans or animals. Some people call it swell head or big head.

"One year we planted a huge field of potatoes and used the crop to feed the hired men and the family. We harvested forty bushels, thinking it was an excellent yield. However, they were all gone by next season. We used them all for the employees and family.

"There were also honeybees on the farm, and the family had a good supply of honey."

"How many horses did you have?" one child asked."We had several working horses and a pair of jackasses to work in the fields."

"*What* did you have?" I asked.

"A jackass is a donkey."

"Really?"

"*Ja*, and that's just what they were too. They were contrary. Sometimes when you wanted them to move, it would sit on its ass."

We all had to laugh and Mother would laugh with us.

Levi said,"That's why they call them jackasses, right, Mom?"

"*Ja.*"

"They have the right name." William started laughing at his own joke.

"What kind of weather did you have?" I asked, changing the subject and hoping to keep the stories going.

Mother looked at the clock and said,"Oh my, it's going on two o'clock and we are still at the dinner table. We'll have to tell that one another time."

"Oh! Come on, we could listen to your stories all afternoon," we all cried.

"Oh! All right."

So another story was told about the weather in Oklahoma. We were all ears, because we enjoyed listening to Mother's stories.

"Well, it was hot in the summer, but we would sometimes have tornadoes. More than what we have here in Iowa.

In fact, one day black clouds were rolling in and when I noticed them I thought I'd better go get William and get ready in case a tornado came. I looked for him through the house and outside in the yard, but I couldn't find him. Keeping my eye on the clouds, I could see a black funnel forming."

Mother continued, "I had started out to the barn to look for your father when I noticed the baby out by the windmill. I ran after him and picked him up and ran for the basement. A little later, I heard emergency vehicles on the roads."

"A newspaper account of April 27, 1942 stated that one hundred people were killed and five hundred injured. A freak tornado struck on that Monday afternoon in the small town of Pryor, not far from our farm. The tornado traveled with gun-barrel straightness down Main Street for a six-block stretch. The power lines were downed; two out of the three hospitals were damaged. Hospitals in neighboring towns were filled with the injured!"

All the local Amish men, including our father helped look for bodies all through the night. By daybreak, three hundred construction workers moved in to help clear the debris and rebuild the town.

We children marveled at this story of faraway destruction and felt lucky not to be living in Oklahoma. Looking back, I think part of my mother's intent must have been to make us feel this way. And it worked!

Elizabeth and I In Foster Homes

Times were so hard after school was out one summer that Mother asked Elizabeth and me if we would go to Aunt Hattie's to stay. We would get room and board in exchange for the chores, including gardening, that we did.

At age six, I agreed to this arrangement, leaving on a Monday and coming home on Saturday. Mother wanted her children home on weekends. It was her way of trying to keep the family together. We girls didn't like going to Aunt Hattie's house, so we agreed to switch off every other week.

The next summer was the same except for one special weekend that I remember. On that weekend, I stayed with Aunt Hattie and Uncle Henry and went to church with them on Sunday. On their way home, they stopped at Mother's house.

Aunt Hattie asked Mother, "Should Alma come along home with us?"

"Do you want to go with them?" Mother asked me.

I nodded my head yes even though I didn't really care to do so. I volunteered to go because I knew my sister Elizabeth would have to go if I didn't. I knew my sister didn't like to go either. So they left, taking me for another week. When we arrived at their homestead, everybody went to do their chores.

I had to clean the eggs, and while I was doing the eggs, I started thinking about home. I longed to be there. Tears began to roll down my cheeks. Suddenly I heard steps entering the room. I tried to wipe my tears so Aunt Hattie wouldn't see that I was crying. She walked over in front of me and asked,"Do you have something in your eye?"

"*Ja*," I lied, trying to give her a smile.

Aunt Hattie left the room. Soon she came back and in an exasperated tone of voice demanded,"Why didn't you say you wanted to stay at home?"

I didn't say a word. I didn't know what to say. All I could do was continue my egg cleaning. I knew the situation at home. What's more, I was a shy and introverted little girl. I never said any more than I had to. Hattie finally left the room when I wouldn't answer her.

Oh, how I longed to be at home whenever I was at Aunt Hattie's house! There were times I wanted to run home, but I knew there were wildcats in the woods. Besides that, I would have to cross the river. I didn't know how to swim, and I was afraid I might fall into the deep part. I was afraid to take the road, because one farmer had several vicious dogs. I also knew Aunt Hattie would really make trouble for me and my mother if I ran away. My fears kept me there, but they didn't stop my tears.

While Elizabeth was taking her turn boarding at Aunt Hattie's, she also had the same emotions. One day, she just couldn't contain her feelings any longer. She saw a horse and buggy coming down the road. She looked and noticed it was one of Mother's lady friends. Elizabeth couldn't resist the opportunity and ran to flag her down.

"May I get a ride home with you?" she begged.

Aunt Hattie saw her and went out to see what Elizabeth was doing by the road.

"Go get in the house, Elizabeth," she ordered.

Elizabeth went to the house, disappointed. She knew she was in trouble. The two ladies visited for about an hour. Then Aunt Hattie came in to see Elizabeth. After their conversation, Elizabeth realized she could never try to leave again. Aunt Hattie just wasn't the understanding type.

The third summer, Mother didn't ask us to go to Aunt Hattie's. Although we didn't complain, she must have seen how we felt. However, our economic situation was still grim, so my mother was always looking for ways to manage with so many children. One day, she came into the house and announced, "Your cousins Daniel Borntrager and William Yoder would like to have two of you children come and stay with them. Daniel, would you like to go to Cousin Daniel's, and, Alma, would you like to go to Cousin William's house?"

"*Ja*," I answered too quickly.

I thought about my experience at Aunt Hattie's, and tears came to my eyes. Daniel nodded his silent approval.

Mother realized we weren't very happy about it and said, "Neither family has any children, and they really would like to have you."

"All right," I agreed again and felt my heart sinking.

The next day, William and Levi had the horse and buggy ready for us. Mother took Daniel and me to our cousins' houses for a week. Mother stopped at Cousin William Yoder's home first and left me there. Then she went to Cousin Daniel Borntrager's to leave Brother Daniel at their place. William Yoder and Daniel Borntrager were neighbors and lived about one mile from our farm.

Cousin Martha was William's wife. She was a petite young woman, about five foot five, with black hair and brown eyes. She was much more sensitive than Aunt Hattie and realized that I was sad and depressed. The third day, she stated, "We'll take a walk over to Cousin Daniel's to see your brother. Would you like that?"

"Oh! *Ja!*" I said. My eyes brightened with surprise, and I gave her a smile.

"All right! Let's go now," she replied, returning my smile. Cousin Martha had hit the nail on the head. I realized then that Martha was going to be all right to live with. I stayed for the summer without wanting to run away.

When school started, I returned home. About a month later, Martha asked Mother, "Could Alma come over every day after school and help me? We are adopting a new baby from Indiana. Since William is building a new farmhouse and will be working late in the evenings, I could use Alma to babysit while I'm doing the evening chores."

At the age of nine I would be allowed to babysit for a newborn! I was overjoyed to go help Martha and stay overnight. Their house was closer to my school, and Martha would pack my lunch every day. Cousin Martha had taken to me as if I were her own daughter. She taught me how to sew with the foot-pedal sewing machine and also how to care for a newborn.

Each evening before Martha went to the barn, she would tell me what to cook for supper and I would have it ready when she finished the chores. I stayed until they moved to their new farm. I couldn't go with them, however, because they had moved into a different school district.

Sickness Strikes

In every Amish home, like any other home, sickness strikes at one time or another. The second year after Father was hospitalized, illness struck our home in the springtime. The old-fashioned measles started with my oldest brother, William, then moved on to Daniel, Junior, Susan, Elizabeth, and myself. Mother pulled all the blinds to keep out the light to protect the children's eyes. It was up to Levi and Mother to maintain the chores for the next several weeks.

Several months later, Daniel awoke complaining of pains in his stomach and side. Mother watched over him all day. In the evening after chores, he said he still didn't feel good but the pain had left. Early the next morning, Mother checked him. She found he had a high fever. His body was becoming green.

According to the Amish religion, no modern conveniences are allowed. No automobiles and, of course, no telephones are permitted. However, my mother knew she had to get help quick for Daniel. She asked William to hop on his horse and hurry over to the modern farmer's house and ask him if he would rush them to the hospital. In the emergency room, Daniel was examined. He was immediately wheeled away, a very sick boy. A nurse came out to get Mother's permission to perform surgery at once.

"What is the problem?" Mother asked.

"It appears to be his appendix; we will have to operate right way," she replied.

Four hours later, the doctor came out to see Mother.

"How is he?" she asked.

"He had a ruptured appendix, and his condition is critical. We did everything we could. Now it's all up to him, but, frankly, it doesn't look good."

"God, he's in your hands now. Please help him. Whatever your will, let it be so," Mother prayed.

Our neighbor, the modern farmer, left the hospital. On his way home, he stopped at the house to inform us other children of our brother's condition. Mother remained at the hospital until Daniel was ready to come home. Due to his youth and strength, he was able to make a rapid recovery. While our mother was away, we children managed the farm unsupervised.

Some years later, both Susan and William also had their appendix removed. However, their operations were more routine and not as critical as in Daniel's case. Susan also had her tonsils removed while she was there.

Amish mothers always breast-feed their babies, if possible. My mother fed her babies this natural way, too. In 1940, I was her sixth newborn baby girl. Mother tried to breast-feed me, but I was a baby who wouldn't take any kind of milk. I cried a lot and Mother didn't know what was wrong with me. Out of her eight babies, she considered me to be the sickliest child of them all. As a child, on many occasions I complained of my ears hurting.

One evening when I was five or six years old, the family had supper at Uncle Judas' home. As usual, I had an earache. Uncle Judas smoked an old pipe. He volunteered to get his pipe hot, and when it was hot, he carefully blew warm smoke into my ears. Next he placed cotton balls in them in an attempt to relieve the pain. This remedy seemed to help temporarily.

One cold winter day, I stayed home from school with a throbbing earache. It was very painful, but I didn't want to complain to Mother. I went upstairs and climbed onto my feather mattress bed. I huddled under the comforter, hiding my pain in tears. Soon Mother discovered I was missing and came upstairs and found me in the unheated room. Mother picked me up and carried me downstairs, sitting me in a living room chair beside the old potbellied stove. She placed a couple of towels to heat on the wood stove and pressed them to my ears. To help relieve the pain, she put a couple of drops of oil in each ear. That Saturday we visited the doctor in Independence.

For years I lived with a constant earache, day in and day out. In the summer of 1950, when I was ten years of age, I was stricken with pneumonia. My illness had affected my hearing also. My brothers and sisters had to shout for me to be able to hear them. In February 1951, I was admitted to the hospital to have my tonsils removed. I was to be released three or four days after surgery. Just prior to the day I was to go home, a tremendous snowstorm raged through the area. Due to road conditions, I was forced to spend another week at the hospital. Before I left, one of the nurses entered my room carrying a newspaper.

"Did you know your name is in the paper?" she asked.

"No, why?"

"The doctor had it put in to let you know what a good patient you have been."

I thought that was really something. It made me happy and I asked in surprise, "Was I?"

"You certainly were," she answered with a smile.

Amish family fishing near Oelwein, Iowa.

Where There Is a Will There Is a Way

One day we younger children were in the kitchen. Mother asked, "Where is Levi?"

"He is outside, in front of the house," I answered. Mother went outside in front of the house to talk to Levi. Soon he came inside and stated, "I'll see if we don't have some meat for the dinner table." He picked up the gun hanging over the door and walked out.

"Hunting season isn't on," Mother called. "I'm going to hunt on our farm." Some hours later, Levi came home with a rabbit to be cooked for dinner.

Most times the cows would come home on their own when it was milking time. One summer evening the cows didn't come, so Levi decided he would go after them on horseback. He rode back through the woods but couldn't locate them. Soon he came back home whistling and smiling as if he were the king of the cowboys.

"Why is he so happy without the cows?" Susan asked.

Sitting high on his horse, Levi walked his steed home through the barnyard up to the house.

"What are you so happy for without the cows?" we asked, watching him.

He dropped something on the front cement slab and smiled. We went over to see what he had.

"Here's something for dinner," he gloated.

"Wow! What a big fish," I remarked.

"How did you get that?" Susan asked.

"I caught it. Will you fix it for supper?"

"*Ja,*" Susan answered with surprise.

"The cows are on the other side of the river, so I have to go get them." He went after the cows, and Susan and Mother cleaned the thirteen-pound fish for dinner. At the supper table, we all wondered how this had come about. How had Levi caught a fish without a fishing pole?

"How did you catch the fish, Levi?" Mother questioned.

"While I let the horse take a drink, I looked down the river and saw two fish coming toward me. I quickly took my shoes off, but I didn't have time to throw my clothes off, so I dived in with my clothes on. I tried to catch both; but one got away. They were very slippery to try to catch with bare hands."

"Boy, it's good fish," Daniel commented."It sure is," everybody agreed. Everyone was proud of their brother.

"Well, where there is a will there is a way," Levi said.

Uncle Judas wouldn't give Mother money for anything. She had to ask him, and then he would turn her down. The boys managed to get two tame rabbits and started to raise them. They had eight rabbit hutches. When they were full, they would turn the rabbits loose on the farm. We had rabbits under the blacksmith shop, corn crib, and buggy shop, and running free all over the yard. It was a pretty sight to see them hippity-hopping from one building to another or just sitting in the driveway or in the yard eating grass.

The boys trained the watchdogs to leave the rabbits alone. When the dogs weren't with the boys, they would sit and watch the rabbits hippity-hopping here and there over the homestead. The boys counted eighty rabbits at one time. When the boys started their rabbit farm, Mother started to raise ducks, too. She started with six ducklings. When the boys had eighty rabbits, she had sixty ducks.

The ducks would waddle down to the creek to swim. It was fascinating to watch them. If they saw something moving under the water as they were swimming, they'd dive down head first and all you could see sticking up was their webbed feet and a perfect curled tail. After a while, some of them would come up on the bank and sun themselves.

It was up to us girls to feed the ducks for Mother. One night, Elizabeth and I were mixing their feed with water at the pump. As we were mixing the meal, the baby ducklings were running under and around our feet. Elizabeth accidentally stepped on one baby duckling, and its eye popped out of its head.

Daniel was walking our way when we saw him and yelled,"Daniel, come quickly!"

He came over and we showed him what had happened. We were afraid Mother would get angry with us. He picked it up, twisted the duck's head off to make sure it wouldn't suffer anymore, and threw it to the pigs. We were upset about it, but he remained calm and said,"Don't worry about it; just try and be more careful."

"All right."

When the feed was ready for the ducks, we would yell out the duck call:"Duckie, Duckie, Duckie, Duck!"

If that wasn't a noisy group coming to the feed trough! Every duck had its own tone, anywhere from high notes to low. I called it a barnyard concert. Fascinated, we'd stand back watching, but sometimes we had to laugh. They'd get up on the tips of their webbed feet, spread their wings out and up, their bodies expanding with air, and then they'd do a ballet dance to their food. It was beautiful but noisy.

When Mother needed money, she would take dressed rabbit, duck, and sometimes chicken to market. This was her way of working around her brother to get cash for what we needed.

The first time we had to dress rabbits, Levi said,"Alma, come help me."

I went outside to help. He caught a rabbit and tied the hind feet up on the fence."Hold the rabbit's ears," he told me.

"Oh, no!" I gasped.

The rabbit looked me in the eye, and I looked back in his. It was just like the rabbit was begging me,"Don't do it; save me!"

"I feel sorry for it," I said.

"Oh, the rabbit won't know what happened. It will be quick?" Levi promised me, and before I knew it, the rabbit was dead. We dressed 3 rabbits to take to market.

We girls had to dress the chickens for her, too. Mother would tell us to go dress three chickens for market. We had a log sitting on its end with two nails on it. I would lay the chicken's head in between the two nails so the head wouldn't move. Then I would take the old ax and cut the head off quickly. I would throw the chicken down on the ground to bleed until it stopped jumping.

The dead chicken was dipped in a bucket of boiling water so I could pluck the feathers.

Susan always held the chickens over flaming papers to burn off the tiny pinfeathers.

One day, Mother said, "Alma, go catch the chickens to dress." Mother was outside and in a hurry.

"Never mind, I'll do it for you," Mother volunteered.

I handed her a chicken. Mother took the chicken's head in her hand and gave it a couple of twists. After the chicken fell to the ground, she threw the severed head into the pigpen.

I was amazed when I realized it was so easy that way. I wouldn't have to look the chicken in the eye when I laid its head on the log. So I tried it and discovered it was easier to do it Mother's way.

When it was time to butcher the ducks, it took more time than the rabbits or chickens. The ducks were beheaded to bleed, and the fine feathers were plucked and saved for pillows and mattresses before dipping the duck into a bucket of boiling water.

One year at Thanksgiving, Mother said, "Dress an extra duck for our Thanksgiving dinner."

"For our Thanksgiving dinner?" I repeated. "*Jah.* They are quite good to eat."

I was surprised, because whenever we dressed a tame rabbit or a duck it was always for market.

We thought it was a treat to have a duck on our Thanksgiving table.

The rabbit skin was also sold for extra cash. So you see it's true-despite Uncle Judas."Where there is a will there is a way."

Electrical Storm

On a calm but hot summer evening, the children had gone upstairs for a good night's sleep. At 1:00 A.M. my mother laid her hand on one of the boy's shoulders. She said, "William, Levi, Daniel, and Junior, wake up. Get up and get dressed."

The boys questioned, "Why?"

"It's storming; we are having an electrical storm," Mom replied.

They didn't argue. When they opened their eyes, the dark night was bright with lightning. Then it would thunder with a loud crack.

Mother went to the girls' room. She shook us awake, mentioning each name. I pulled the covers up over myself, stating, "I don't want to get up. I want to sleep."

Mother came back and shook me again. "Get up."

"Why? I'm tired."

At that moment, it cracked hard. I jumped out of bed, put my dress on, and ran downstairs to the living room. When I entered the room, the boys were sitting on the davenport. Daniel was wide awake with fear, and Levi was nodding his head with his eyelids too heavy to keep them open. Since William was the oldest, he was awake, waiting in case he had to help Mother with the responsibilities. Susan and Elizabeth were asleep on the daybed, and Mother was sitting in a kitchen chair in the living room facing the window. She said, "Come sit down."

"Why do we always have to get up when it storms?"

I sat beside Mother where I could watch the storm. The outside was as dark as the ace of spades. You couldn't even see the building twenty feet away from the house. The next minute lightning would flash and the lightning would be so bright you could see the neighbors' homestead a mile across the field.

Each time it thundered extra hard, we would jump. Mother would get up from her chair, walk to the window, and check every building on the farm, and the neighbors' buildings within sight. Then she would sit back with relief.

Mother wanted us to understand why we had to get up every time there was a storm. She sat up in her chair at attention and proceeded to tell us how they had had a storm in Kansas.

"When my folks lived in Kansas, we had all gone to bed on a hot summer night. No indication of a storm was in sight. During the night an electrical storm appeared. Grandpa awoke about 2:00 A.M. He noticed a continuous flickering of light outside. He got up to check it and went to the window. Without hesitation he grabbed his pants and yelled at the boys upstairs, 'William, David, Judas, Henry, the barn is on fire!'

"Hastily the boys grabbed their pants and in their bare feet ran to help save the animals. Their sisters hurried to help pump water at the hand pump.

"The window along the stairway had broken from the heat of hot flames, and glass had fallen over the stairs. The boys ran heedlessly through the broken glass lying on the stairway.

"The cows, calves, horses, and a couple of sows with piglets had been left in the barn for the night. The boys ran into the burning barn to get the cows and horses out. They had to lead them out one by one. The barn was so hot they had to fight the last couple of cows to get them out to safety. They led them to a corral away from the barn.

"Grandpa was trying to get the calves out. Burning pieces of ceiling started to drop here and there. They turned the horses loose. When they thought they had everything out, someone said, 'We forgot one cow and calf in a stall.'

"'Oh, no!' Grandpa ran for the barn once more.

"Neighbors started arriving. They had seen the flames from miles away and were coming over to help. Everyone yelled, 'Don't go back in; that barn's going to collapse!'

"It was too late; Grandpa had disappeared back into the flames.

"The cows were wild. The boys were still struggling to get them into a corral. The cows wanted to run back into the burning barn.

"Grandpa had to struggle with the cow to get it out. He had to leave the calf behind, because he couldn't get to it. He emerged from the barn beating the flames from his shoulders as he narrowly missed being struck by a falling beam.

"Everybody was relieved to see him safe. The neighbors and friends were pumping water into buckets and passing them down a line hand to hand. The water was poured over the buildings close to the barn. Every time they threw water on the building, it would sizzle, with steam rolling into the sky. They all worked hard trying to save the other buildings.

"The cow Grandpa saved had received third degree burns on her back. Before they had her in the corral, she started to run for the barn-back into the burning inferno. They couldn't stop her. She burned with the barn.

"Grandpa was sick at heart to see the animal burn alive. The sows with piglets and a calf were trapped inside and burned to ashes."

I asked, "Did they get everything else out of the barn?"

"No, all the equipment in the barn plus the hay went up in flames. By 7:00 A.M. the barn was completely destroyed. Nothing but hot coals remained, and these smoked for days and days. Friends and neighbors left around 7:00 A.M., when they weren't needed to pour any more water.

"Grandpa and the boys returned to the house exhausted. They washed their feet on the porch. A couple of the boys complained that their feet hurt. When they washed them, they noticed they were cut."

"How did they get cut?" I asked.

"When they ran over the broken glass on the stairway," Mom replied.

"Did they rebuild the barn?"

"Of course. Before all the friends left, they asked Grandpa to get the estimate together to rebuild the barn.

Amish don't have insurance on their buildings with an insurance company like a lot of people do today.

"The Amish don't subscribe to insurance through a regular insurance company. It is not in accordance with their beliefs. Therefore, they have their own private insurance.

"If a barn is destroyed by fire or other means, they get an estimate for material needed to replace it and then everyone gets together and in one day they rebuild it. The other families furnish three-fourths of the expenses for the material, and the women bring food along to feed the seventy-five to one hundred men needed for the one day job."

"What did they do when it was time to milk the cows?"

"After breakfast the boys went out to the workshop and made themselves a one-footed milking stool. Then they milked the cows out in the open of the corral until the barn was rebuilt, rain or shine."

"They really milked the cows out in the open?" I asked.

"*Ja.* There was no barn; where else would they milk?"

"Oh! *Ja.*"

"The storm has calmed down, so why don't you all go back to bed now 'til morning?"

"*Ja.*" Everybody agreed and was ready to go back to bed again.

After morning chores were done, it was daylight. Daniel had walked in from the barn and noticed a split in the house foundation. He entered the house, saying, "Mom! Remember last night we thought it sounded like the house got hit?"

"*Ja.*"

"Well, there's a split in the foundation. Lightning must have hit it."

We all had to go out and investigate.

"That was a close one, wasn't it, Mom?" Daniel asked.

"It sure was and a noisy one, too."

We were thankful to God for keeping us in his hands throughout the night.

Billy Goat Rough

As per the slogan of the postal service, through rain or sleet the mailman always got through and arrived at our house, usually at the dinner hour. This day he blew his horn several times.

"Go see what the mailman wants, William," Mother called.

Soon William came in and told Mother, "The mailman has a billy goat and wonders if we want it. He can't keep it in town where he lives. We can have the goat if we give him a good home."

"A billy goat?" she gasped.

"*Ja!* May we have it?"

"Oh, I don't think so."

"Please, Mom. Let us have it, please. We have enough room here on the farm," William begged.

All the children were surprised and helped him, begging Mother to please let us have the goat.

"How would we get it here?" Mom asked."I'll go ask," William replied.

William went out and asked the mailman. He came back to the house and said, "He will bring it out tomorrow afternoon."

"All right," Mother replied.

We were all very excited at the prospect of having a new pet, and it seemed we discussed it every waking moment until the next day.

The next day, at about 1:00 P.M., the mailman honked his horn again and we ran to see who it was. There was Billy in the backseat of the mailman's car. The mailman got out of the car, opened the back door, and pulled Billy from the car.

There he was, our new pet, horns and all. He was a buff-colored goat with eight-inch horns. The mailman expressed his appreciation to us for taking Billy and giving him a good home. Then he departed down the dusty road.

As the dust cleared, we stood there inspecting our new pet, who looked like he had just lost his best friend. This depression didn't last long for Billy, though. He was soon keeping us all alarmed and entertained with his devilish ways.

Susan always disappeared after dinner. She tried to get out of doing dishes. After dinner, she would take off for the outhouse. She would sit there for an hour or two looking through the wish book (the Sears catalog), wishing.

One day I decided to go with her. As we were walking to the outhouse, Susan noticed the billy goat and shouted, "Run, Alma, the billy goat's coming toward us!" We took off running as fast as our feet could carry us. Susan had a couple of crackers in her hand. The crackers flew up in the air and down on the ground. The goat saw them and stopped to check and eat them while we scrambled to the outhouse.

"Boy, that was close!" I stated with relief.

"It's a good thing I had those crackers in my hand. But how are we going to get back to the house? I don't have any more crackers to give him."

"I don't know, but he's a mean one." My sisters and I were all secretly afraid of Billy.

We waited and waited for the goat to leave the area. We watched him through a crack in the door. Then we looked through the wish book, hoping he would leave. After an hour, the goat started out toward the barn.

"Oh, he's going for the barn," Susan whispered.

I looked out to see if he was far enough away so we could make a run for the house. Then the stupid animal stopped and gazed back at the outhouse, looking for us. We waited a little longer as the goat turned toward the barn, walking like he had given us up.

"Run, Alma, as fast as you can go!" Susan ordered.

"All right."

We both took off running as fast as we could, up the hill to the house.

"Here he comes!" Susan yelled as she gasped for breath.

Susan opened the door to run inside and tripped over the steps and fell on her stomach on the porch floor. I saw the goat behind me and jumped over her. Still lying on the floor, Susan pulled up her knees so I could slam the door. After we were safe, we both started laughing. We laughed so hard that Mother heard us. She came to the door and questioned,"What's going on out here?"

Susan picked herself up off the floor, and we both explained what had happened. Mother laughed at us.

As we walked into the kitchen, all the dirty dishes were still waiting to be washed. It never failed; the dishes were always there for us girls no matter how long we were gone.

One day, Brother Daniel was walking to the barn to do his evening chores. When he was close to the barn, he turned around and saw the billy goat. Daniel stood there, eye to eye with the goat, watching him to see what he was going to do. As he stood there, the billy goat came running toward him. Daniel kept his brown eyes on him and stood still. Just before the goat was going to ram him, he put his head down and closed his eyes to let Daniel have it. Daniel stepped to his right, and the goat ran into the barn head-on. The goat was surprised and shook his head with pain. But that wasn't enough; he started after Daniel again.

Daniel ran and leaped inside the barn and closed the door, causing Billy to crash against it. Daniel had to laugh, because the joke was on Billy again.

One spring morning, the brothers came in for breakfast after chores were all done. William and Daniel were washing their face and hands in the separator room. Levi was walking into the kitchen, where Mom was trying to get the pancakes done. The sisters were setting the table and trying to have everything ready for breakfast.

Levi asked, "Mother, may I make a harness for the goat?"

"Are there enough scraps of leather in the blacksmith shop to make one?"

"I have to check but I think so."

"If you can find enough, go ahead."

A week later, Levi had a harness made and William had the little red wagon ready. They hitched the goat to the wagon and gave rides to the little ones.

Levi was the master of the goat. He wasn't afraid of it, and the goat knew it, too.

"May I have a ride, Levi?" I asked. "Sure! Come and get in the wagon."

I was all excited and climbed on the wagon to go for the ride. During the ride, I asked, "May I drive him?"

"Sure, if you want to," he said and handed me the reins. I took the reins and when they were in my hands, the goat immediately stopped. Billy turned his head back and looked at me, and I looked at Billy. I ordered him to go, but he just stood there looking at me. This scared me, so I said, "Here, take the reins; he knows that it's not you." I handed Levi the reins.

Levi took the reins, laughing while he drove me back to the house.

"That's fun, but I don't think Billy likes me," I commented.

"He knows who is boss."

Levi enjoyed his new pet, but it didn't take us long to discover why the mailman didn't want Billy. Billy brought plenty of excitement to the farm.

Bottomless Hole

The Amish tradition is to welcome a new family when they move in from another settlement. Word was passed on in church on Sunday that a new family had bought a local farm about four and a half miles from our farm.

This family had moved to our dry state of Iowa in the spring. The Amish try to move either after crops had been harvested or before fields were planted.

At the dinner table, Mother stated, "I want to go to welcome the Amish family that moved in from Ohio. Too much time has passed already, and I must do it today before we make our second hay for the season. The hay is cut already, and when I get back we'll make hay."

Levi asked, "May I go along, because I heard they have a boy my age?"

"*Ja!* That would be a good idea."

It was on a hot summer day in August that Mother and son arrived at the new family's homestead. Mother introduced Levi and herself, and the newcomers did the same. Mother visited with the folks while Levi visited with their son, Abe.

Through their conversation, Abe learned that Levi lived on a farm with a river running across and through the woods a quarter-mile from his house.

Abe asked, "Are there any deep spots where you can go swimming?"

"Yeah! A couple of deep spots. In fact, one day we were making fences and we wanted to go across this one place, so I dived in to see how tall a fence post we would need. I couldn't find bottom. We had to change our fence line."

"Do you have to make a fence across that river?"

"Why, sure! If we want to keep the cows from going onto our neighbors' land. When the season is dry, like right

99

now, the river is low and calm, and we can wade across with a horse and buggy in some places. The water is so clear, we can see bottom all the way across it, except for the deep part. The deep part makes good fishing."

"Boy, you are lucky. This farm is dry, no ponds or nothing. Just a water well."

"But it's good for farming."

Abe had to agree. "Do you think we could go swimming tonight after hay making and the other chores are done?" he asked.

"Do you know how to swim?"

"Oh, *ja!* I sure would like to wash the hay dirt and sweat off after this hot sun goes down."

"I agree. We swim almost every day in the summer. We don't care if you come over, as long as you know how to swim. Come on over; it will be refreshing."

Mother called, "Levi, it is time to go now."

Levi was excited. He had found a new friend and was going swimming. Abe came over in the evening, after his work was done.

Since the Amish family was new, they didn't know all the traditions yet. Iowa was different from other Amish settlements.

As Abe walked with my brothers to the river, they began to inform Abe what the local Amish attitudes were. "The Amish here don't want us to go swimming. Let us tell you something that happened with the church about a year ago. We always went swimming, either in the river or the creek behind the barn. One day, at 105 degrees, it was so hot we decided to take a swim in the creek to cool off. We threw our clothes on shore and dived in, in our birthday suits. We never had a swimming suit. To own a swimming suit is against the Amish religion here. It's not considered modest.

"While we were swimming we heard a horse and buggy cross the little wooden bridge. It was about fifty feet from the water hole where we were swimming. Trees and high weeds grew between us. We swam to the far north side so we wouldn't be seen. As the buggy followed the curve in the road, they could look down on the south side of the creek and see our clothes, lying in the open on the shore.

"Next Sunday we had church. We all went to church unaware of any trouble. When we got there, it was announced that there was a meeting being held for the members after service. After service, all the children were excused. Now was the time for all the busybodies that liked to make rules to get busy. Our mother was not aware the meeting was for her benefit.

"The meeting started with, 'One of the members saw Katie's boys' clothes laying on the creek bank.' Some parents started to whisper with astonished expressions. A voice came from the crowd and said, 'Katie, do you have anything to say to this?'

"'No.' She sat thinking, it was hard to believe this meeting was because her boys went swimming in their own farm's creek.

"'Do you realize those boys didn't have any clothes on? That is a sin.'

"'Boys will be boys.'

"'They are your boys and you are responsible for them.'

"'I agree.'

"'Well, what are you going to do about it?'

"'What do you want me to do about it?'

"'You should confess your sins.'

"'I didn't do it.'

"'They are your boys.'

"'I can't keep my eyes on them every minute.' Again she sat thinking. *They didn't hurt anybody; they minded their own business. This is ridiculous. The boys work hard to help me farm. They work like men instead of boys. Why did I ever agree to move to Iowa six years ago? Nothing but problems from several nosy women who like to pick, pick, pick.*

"Forty-five minutes passed. Our mother finally made a confession just to keep peace with them, so they wouldn't throw her out of the church. She also wanted to be a good example to us. After the meeting, dinner was served and we left. On the way home, Mother told the story about the

101

meeting. After this public chastisement, Mother made sure that any swimming we did was kept a secret among our family members."

As the boys walked toward the swimming hole, Levi cautioned, "So, Abe, you make sure you don't tell anyone about going swimming."

"Oh! I won't."

When they arrived at the river, Abe said, "Where is the bottomless hole?"

"Right over there," The boys started taking their heavy, homemade clothes off.

"You have never hit bottom here?"

"*Nah!* Never."

"That's hard to believe-never hit bottom!" He jumped in with excitement and the boys followed. A little later, they came up to the surface.

"Boy, this is great!" Abe said.

Levi and William had to agree. They swam like a couple of fish in the sea for a while.

One by one they all climbed out and sat on the bank. Relaxed, Abe exclaimed, "It really feels good to be clean!"

They all had to agree on this ninety-seven-degree evening. Abe was on cloud nine. He really was enjoying himself. Levi and William noticed that he didn't swim as well as they did, but he was having a good time.

Abe asked, "I   want to try to hit bottom. Do you care?"

William and Levi agreed to stay out on the bank with Abe's pocket watch.

Abe dove down and disappeared. Levi and William waited and waited, keeping their eyes on the pocket watch and the bottomless hole.

Levi asked, "William, what do you think? Several minutes have passed."

"Give him a little more time."

However, when a minute passed, Levi stated, "I'm going after him. I just know he's having trouble. You stay here, William, because I'm a faster swimmer."

He dove in and was gone for a while. A little later he came backup to check and asked, "Did he come back up?"

102

"Nah."

Levi dived back down. Farther and farther he went. He couldn't find Abe! Levi came up to check for the second time to see if he missed Abe. When Levi came to the surface, he looked at William worriedly.

William volunteered, "He hasn't come back up yet."

Levi took a quick dive back down. He continued searching the water, looking for Abe for a third time. He knew he had to keep his cool, for he couldn't panic or they all would be in real trouble. He continued down, hoping to find Abe. Levi knew Abe hadn't floated up, so he had to be somewhere down deeper. He continued to go down even faster. His eyes were wide open so he wouldn't miss Abe along the way. Levi was getting worried, knowing Abe was in real trouble. He swam straight down, feeling like a fish and knowing he had no time to waste. Every second was crucial for Abe as well as himself. He was getting more and more worried. "A little deeper," he coaxed himself, swimming faster.

"Come on, Abe, where are you?" he said to himself. "I have to find you!"

Levi began to worry about how deep he was going, but his worry for Abe kept him swimming downward. He started to plead with himself, "Don't give up; you just can't give up." Continuing down, he felt himself desperate for air.

However, as Levi swam down farther, he spotted a body and swam over to it. Abe saw Levi and, desperate for help, grabbed him and started to pull Levi down with him. Levi struggled with the drowning Abe.

Abe was gasping for air as they struggled. Levi tried to pull him up, but Abe wanted to go the wrong way. Levi tried to pull him up toward the surface. Abe pulled him under again. They struggled violently. Levi was gasping for air. He was determined and strong, continuing to struggle to pull Abe to the surface.

From the bank, William kept his eyes open and looked for any signs of them in the water. He could see deep into the river, for the water was very clear. He was getting nervous, waiting and thinking, *Where are they both? Come on, you guys.* He knew they both had to be desperate for air at that point. Time passed. However, he couldn't wait any longer. Panic-stricken, he dived into the bottomless hole and went down swimming like a fish. Anxiously, he scanned the water to find his brother and friend. Eyes wide open, he swam farther down. He saw them struggling. He swam over to help Levi. Abe grabbed William, too, pulling him under. William broke loose, swam behind Abe, and knocked Abe out cold. William and Levi both grabbed an arm and swam to the surface. Dragging Abe onto the bank, Levi fell exhausted to the ground and inhaled fresh air with relief.

William worked on Abe, pushing on his body to get the water out of him. Then they all rested in silence.

Levi broke the silence. "Abe, what happened?"

"I lost my sense of direction. I thought Levi was taking me the wrong way."

"Do you realize that I almost drowned down there trying to help you? You pulled me under and put up a fight like that. We are both very lucky that I was a better swimmer and stronger than you. I should have knocked you out."

"You are supposed to knock out the person that you are trying to save so he can't fight back," interrupted William. "They will pull you under if you don't."

"Boy! We are both lucky. Thanks, William, for coming to help me. I don't think I could have made it without you."

Abe was very apologetic and thanked them both. "I will never try to find the bottom of this hole again, because it doesn't have one."

They all dressed and went home with memories of an experience they would never forget.

Mischief

My mother made frequent trips to Independence. Mother probably made more trips than the average parent because our father was hospitalized in Independence.

When Mother went to town on errands and left us children behind unattended, it gave us the opportunity to be mischievous. Mother always said,"What one child doesn't think of the other one will." How right she was on that!

Saturday was usually a day for cleaning and baking. It was also the day when Mother made her trip to town. One Saturday after dinner, Levi was riding his horse around the farm. We didn't have saddles, so the boys always rode bareback.

Levi rode his horse up to the house, and one of us children said,"Do you think a horse could walk up the stairway?"

"Don't know."

"Want to try it?"

"Yeah."

"Does everybody agree not to tell Mom?" Levi asked.

"*Ja!* We agree."

"Okay, but you make sure you don't say a word to Mom."

We placed a younger child at the window to watch for Mother in case she should come home before we managed to get the horse back out.

The horse was brought in through the porch, the separator room, and through the kitchen to the stairway. As he started into the stairway, the horse lifted his tail.

"Oh! He's going to go in the house!" Susan gasped."Get the dustpan quick!" Daniel ordered.

I grabbed the dustpan and handed it to Susan. She took it, but the horse had gas.

"WOW! What a smell!" I said, holding my nose.

Levi was trying to coax the horse to go up the stairs. He had taken six steps and wouldn't go any farther.

"What's the holdup?" Susan asked.

"He's stuck. I can't get him up or down!" Levi complained.

The little one at the window yelled, "Mom's coming, Mom's coming!"

"Oh, *na!* Get that horse out of here quick!" Susan screamed.

"I'm trying, but I can't get him up or down. Stand back. I'll try to scare him back down!" Levi shouted.

He lifted his arms up quickly and scared the horse back down and let the horse outside. As Levi led him out, Susan followed with the bucket of water, mopping behind them. Susan had just finished mopping the kitchen floor when Mother pulled up in front of the house.

"Come here, William," Mother called.

William picked a watermelon out of the buggy and carried it to the water pump to place it in cold water for our treat.

"Boy! Mom got us a watermelon!" I said to Susan with surprise.

"Did she!"

"*Ja*"

"Did you get your work done?" Mother asked.

"*Ja*, but the kitchen floor is still wet," Susan answered.

After all the evening chores were finished, we enjoyed the special treat Mother had brought home for us. This was unusual, since she had never done it before.

On the following Tuesday evening, a buggyful of Amish men came over to see Mother.

"Mother, what do the men want?" we asked.

"Stay out of the living room; it's about the watermelon that I bought last Saturday."

We stayed out to leave Mother alone, since we knew she was depressed and troubled. When the men left, we asked, "How do they know about the watermelon?"

"Your cousin William Yoder saw me and offered to carry the watermelon to the buggy. On his way home, he stopped to see Uncle Judas and told him that he saw me. William told me he didn't think anything about it. But Judas said the melon was something that wasn't necessary to buy. That's why they came over to see me."

Mother had left the living room to go to the kitchen to get away from the men. When she started back to the living room, she stopped and looked at the gun hanging over the doorway. She thought, *How I would like to use that gun on myself; then I wouldn't be a burden to anyone anymore. But what would my poor children do without me? Suicide isn't the answer.*

We children had really enjoyed that frivolous watermelon, and Mother's heart had rejoiced to see her children so happy.

I have to wonder what the Amish would have said back then if they knew what we children really did sometimes. We tried to overcome our boring life at home. No matter how much responsibility children are given, they still have to have some fun. Kids will be kids. We didn't have a box of toys to choose from. The girls in this settlement were not to have dolls that resembled real babies. They had to be rag dolls, dressed in Amish clothes. This was the Amish way of keeping their children from taking an interest in other dress styles as they grew up.

To have some fun, the boys made themselves stilts to walk on. Daniel built a tunnel through the hay in the haymow. I can recall we were playing in the hay and every child had to crawl through the tunnel. When we were crawling through and were deep in the hay there was little air.

"I can't breathe," I said quickly. "I can't either," Elizabeth replied.

We all had to crawl backward to get back out. The opening was just big enough to crawl through. When everyone went in, it cut off the air supply. I advised the other children later not to try to go into a hay tunnel unless there were two openings for the air to circulate. Otherwise, your life could be in danger.

One day while Mother was gone, we children were home unsupervised. After dinner, William, age seventeen, and Levi, age sixteen, were in a mischievous mood.

Levi said, "I wonder if a chicken would drink beer or even get drunk on the stuff?"

"Don't know," said William, "but let's try it and see."

"*Ja.*"

They went back to the buggy and took a bottle out and opened it. Daniel caught a banty rooster for them. Levi took the rooster and poured beer down its throat, a little at a time. Then he let it go. The banty wobbled back and forth. It was a comical sight to see a drunken rooster. We all had our fun for that day, and the experiment also satisfied our curiosity.

Mother told us a story of how she had given pigs some beer when she was a teenager. She said that the pigs were smarter than people.

We asked her, "Why?"

"The pigs wouldn't even drink the stuff," she replied.

"That's pretty bad stuff if a pig doesn't even drink it." This was Mother's way to tell the boys that beer was not good for them. She had seen the sixpack in their buggy.

Sometimes we would ask Mother how she knew what we were doing when she had her back turned toward us.

"I have eyes in the back of my head," she would say with a smile.

"No, you don't," we would say. But there were times when we thought she really did.

Hunting Season

One year when hunting season opened, the boys naturally wanted to go hunting. At the breakfast table, William asked, "May I go hunting?"

Mother replied, "When you go hunting, you have to be very careful. I don't want anyone outside when you take that gun outdoors."

"Why?" both boys asked.

"Because that's how your grandpa died."

"Watcha mean?"

Sitting at the table, Mother told us another story.

"Grandpa always had a rule that the gun wasn't to be used on a Sunday. On Sundays he always slept in and the boys did the chores without him. One Sunday morning, a flock of blackbirds covered the trees and ground behind the barn. My brother Daniel went to the house to get the gun and checked to see if Grandpa was still in bed. 'Grandpa wasn't seen up yet,' I told him. Daniel took the gun and went out behind the barn. While my brother took the gun out, Grandpa had gotten dressed and walked out to the pigpen to survey the homestead. My brother shot at a bird and hit a tree branch. He heard a scream and ran to check to see what was wrong. He found Grandpa on the ground. He screamed for help: 'I shot Dad! I shot Dad!'

"Everybody came running. Mom sent one boy to the neighbors to go for help on horseback. While he went for help, the other brothers carried Grandpa to the yard. Grandma asked me to get him a chair. I ran and got it, and they sat him in the chair to wait for help to arrive. He was rushed to the hospital, and they operated on him. The bullet had just missed his heart. Three weeks later, he wanted to come home, so he was discharged from the hospital. However, his condition still wasn't very good.

Several months later, my brother's glass of water was sitting on the table. Grandma wanted to get him a clean glass of water, but Grandpa said, 'No, I want a drink out of my son's glass.' After he had his drink of water, he died.

"We believe that was his way of saying he loved his son and wanted there to be peace between them. Daniel was forgiven."

"How long did Grandpa live after he was shot?" we asked.

"He lived for six months. My brother didn't kill him, but he shortened Grandpa's life. Daniel always blamed himself for killing Grandpa."

"How old were you?" I asked.

"I was nine years old."

"What happened to Grandma then?" one of us asked.

"Later my mother met a gentleman who wanted to marry her, and they were married. When my mother decided to marry him, we told her we didn't know if we could call him Dad. But as time went by, he was so good to Mom and us that before we knew it we were calling him Dad. Then they took a trip to the Colorado mountains and on their trip Mother took sick. When they came home, she went to the doctor's. We learned that she had cancer. She died a year later.

"What did your stepfather do then?" I asked.

"Well, his home had been in Plain City, Ohio, so he decided to go back to be with his children."

"What? Did he leave you in Kansas?"

"He asked us unmarried children to go with him. Actually, everyone was married except Brother Daniel and myself. My older sister said, 'You're not leaving with him,' but Daniel decided he was going regardless of what she said. I stayed with my sister, because my sister thought it didn't look right for me to go along."

Following this recital of family history and tradition, we all left the breakfast table and William stated, "I won't be hunting around the buildings."

"All right; be careful," Mother replied.

We had the same rule at our house-the gun was never to be taken out on Sundays. Every time the gun was taken behind the barn for target practice, the boys would warn us not to leave the house.

One day after school, we saw several strangers hunting across the road in the field.

Daniel said, "I'm going to check if they have permission." He rode up to them on the horse bareback.

When he arrived, he didn't know them, and so he asked, "Did you have any luck today?"

They answered, "Yes."

Daniel asked, "Did you get permission to hunt here?"

"No, but we went over our limit with this rabbit we just shot. Why don't you take it?"

"No, that's all right; I don't want to take it from you."

"That's okay. You take it home for dinner." And one stranger handed Daniel the rabbit.

"Thank you!"

Then the hunters departed and Daniel rode back to the farm. On his way back, his horse spooked and started to run wild. When he came to a sharp curve in the road, Daniel tried to hang onto the horse and the rabbit flew out of his hand into the air. The horse ran so fast that Daniel barely made it into the driveway. When the horse arrived at the barn door, he made a sudden stop. He was huffing and puffing and acting wild. Patting him, Daniel coaxed the horse to settle down. Then he jumped off and put him away for the night. We had seen him on the running horse and ran out to see if he was all right.

We asked, "What happened?"

"Those guys gave me a rabbit. The horse smelled the blood, and when a horse smells blood he goes wild."

"Where's your rabbit?"

"I lost it on the curve, trying to hang onto the horse. I'm going down and see if I can find it."

He returned shortly with the rabbit, and it was dressed and put in salt water to soak overnight.

Arthur, Illinois

The Missing Dresses

Mom's oldest brother, Uncle Henry, was an average-built man with medium dark brown hair, a quiet gentleman married to a woman named Hattie. She wore the pants in their house. She even tried to boss everyone in the church numerous times concerning our family and the dress code of the Amish.

I believe Aunt Hattie would even have enjoyed taking her husband's place as preacher. However, the Amish tradition is that women are to be silent during church service. Following the service, however, the business meeting was opened to all members of the congregation. Hattie would always have her say and argue if everyone didn't agree with her. She was a pushy busybody.

Mother had just made new dresses for my sister and me. This was a treat, because we usually got new dresses only twice a year. This was a big event for a young Amish girl.

We pulled the ankle-length dresses over our heads, pinning the front opening shut and feeling the little mandarin collar and the long loose sleeves. They were beautiful dresses. For church, we covered them with a white organza cape and an apron. A V-shaped cape was pulled over our heads and pinned at the waist in the back. In front the cape crisscrossed to the waistline and was pinned down with straight pins. The apron pinned on around the waist. A ribbon was tied around the neck so the cape was folded over and around the ribbon to hold the cape in place.

From pictures, I knew this was how early American women dressed. Yet this was 1950. We were Amish and we were still dressing like pioneer women.

Sewing day was that one day a month when women from the church gathered to sew. This particular month, they had chosen our house, to help Mother. Mother told the

113

children the women were coming to help with the sewing that day. When my sister Susan heard they were coming, she ran upstairs to hide her dating dress in the old trunk. A dating dress was a dress to wear when going out with boys. Susan knew her dress didn't conform to the dress code because she had made the hem to fall three inches below the knee instead of being ankle-length. Normally I wasn't in a hurry to get home from school, because I dreaded all those chores. But today I couldn't wait to get home because it was sewing day. When school was out, I didn't wait for my brothers and sisters. I took off skipping and running for home. A tomboy, I would rather walk the two and one-half miles than ride anyway. I was hoping I would have something new made for me when I got home. Thinking realistically, I knew I probably wouldn't, since I had a new dress already.

I arrived home about the same time as the others. We girls raced upstairs to change into working clothes, hoping there might be a surprise for us. My oldest sister thumbed through her dresses hanging on her peg. We younger girls did the same thing. We couldn't find anything new. Then Susan checked the old trunk for her dating dress that she liked so much. Instead she found her dress gone. Elizabeth and I noticed our new dresses were gone, too.

"Someone took my dress," Susan cried. "Ours are gone, too," Elizabeth and I cried in unison. Mother had quietly slipped upstairs and was standing in the doorway with an apologetic look on her face. "Your Aunt Hattie went through the clothes. I'm sorry."

"She took our dresses. Why?"

"She said the material was too worldly and against church rules, so she took them."

We couldn't believe it. It was hard for Mother to keep us in clothes. We had been hoping we would have something new when we came home. Instead, we not only didn't find anything new, but we found our new dresses that we had had been taken from us. It was hard enough for Mother to keep eight children in clothes without having anything taken away from us. Mother had ordered the material from a mail order catalog. The green material had a frosty look to it. We didn't see anything wrong with it. It was plain-not printed or patterned.

Mother sympathized with her three girls. "Don't worry. I'll see somehow that you get new dresses. Now go do your chores."

Mother tried not to show it, but she was sad and upset.

"Oh! Hattie makes me mad; she has no business going through our things," Susan complained.

"I don't like her at all!" All three sisters agreed on this point. The busybodies were working in the living room. Mother had gone back to finish what the women were working on.

Elizabeth and I went downstairs and outside, away from the busy women. We were upset and didn't want to see them. The other children went about doing their chores, wishing the visiting women would leave.

While Elizabeth and I were loading our arms full with firewood to carry to the house, Elizabeth stated, "I wish they would all leave."

"*Ja.* I can't stand them," I replied, with an angry feeling inside. When everybody had left, we went inside.

Susan asked, "Mom, what did the women sew today?"

"They made pants for the boys."

"Why did Aunt Hattie have to go through our clothes then?"

"I don't know."

"Oh! Those dummie people," I complained.

"They just had to stick their noses in our things, didn't they?" Susan shouted in tears, continuing, "I wish they would mind their own business. Aunt Hattie is so afraid I'm going to look too good for the young fellows. Well, she doesn't have to worry, because with the styles here it's impossible to look good. No matter how hard you try. She's always sticking her nose where it doesn't belong. I'd like to cut it off for her."

"So would I," I agreed.

"Me, too," Elizabeth added.

115

Our poor mother. She was caught in between. She wouldn't argue with us; she knew we were upset and had every right to be. There were times when she didn't know which way to turn. She would say, "Where there is a will there is a way." This was the family's saying as we tried to go forward instead of giving up.

The day after sewing day, Mother stated, "Alma, Aunt Hattie said she would pay you a dollar a week when you work for her in the summer." When I had enough weeks in to earn the material, Aunt Hattie went and bought the material and gave it to my mother. Mother said, "Aunt Hattie gave me the material for your new dresses."

I wanted to see it right away to see what color she had bought. When I saw it, I was so surprised. "Red?" I asked. "She got us that?"

"*Ja*."

"I thought we weren't allowed to have red?"

"Well! So did I," Mother answered.

Aunt Hattie asked Mother how we liked our dresses. Mother told her what I had said. Aunt Hattie asked if the material was red. Mother said, "*Ja*.." Aunt Hattie had thought it was dark purple. When Mother told us this, we had to laugh. We were told that we weren't allowed to have red or white dresses. Red is evil and white is for purity. There is only one that is pure-Jesus. Mother made our dresses for school and we didn't say any more about the color. We knew Mother wouldn't get in trouble for buying the red material.

Later on, I asked Mother, "What did Hattie do with the green dresses?"

"She made me mail them to your cousins in Ohio."

"Oh! Okay."

And the subject was dropped.

Old-fashioned Winter

Our winters in Iowa in those days of the 1940's seemed rough. It seemed to me then that when we got our first snowfall, it would always snow for at least two days. The second night, I remember standing at the window watching the snowflakes fall. Work on a farm doesn't stop because of inclement weather. It's just like the slogan of the postal service. "Neither rain nor snow nor gloom of night will keep us from our appointed rounds."

The older boys did the milking morning and night. After school, my sister Elizabeth, just fourteen months younger than myself, helped me with the firewood. It was in big chunks and had to be chopped for use in our stoves. The finer the wood, the more quickly it catches fire.

A couple of wagonloads of logs were stored under our large walnut trees, and the ax was next to the woodpile. I would stand a log on end and cut it into two pieces. If it was a very large log, I would split it into four pieces. This was one of my favorite chores. I was a tomboy and liked the outdoors. As I cut the logs, my sister gathered up the pieces and carried an armload to the woodbox. There'd be one box beside the stove in the kitchen and one beside the heating stove in the living room.

We didn't think much about this then-it was an accepted thing that everyone did. But in later years, I realized that this was what the pioneers did as they carved out the new frontiers in our country. Yet at the time I was doing this old-fashioned chore, our country had forty-eight states and was civilized and modernized.

Carrying wood was done every day-summer and winter. We carried more in winter to keep two stoves going. In summer, we'd carry wood for our cook stove.

It fell upon the girls to carry the water, too. From the house out back, down a small hill, between the pigpen and chicken house, we'd cross the cement wall at the steps, yet still had to go downhill to the pump.

In winter we could slide down on packed snow, but slippery snow made it that much harder to climb up with full buckets. On this day, Elizabeth and I had filled our buckets with water and started back up the hill to the house. However, before we reached the top of the hill, Elizabeth slipped and fell. The buckets went tumbling back down. I tried not to laugh, but it was too comical so I had to let out a laugh. I missed the buckets coming at me and slipped down the hill as well. Elizabeth was angry and tried to pick herself up with her ankle-length dress tangled up around her legs.

"Oh! So dumm," I said. I tried to get up, saying, "Jack and Jill went down the hill to fetch a pail of water; Jack fell down and broke his crown, and Jill came tumbling after." Elizabeth and I both broke out in laughter, trying to see humor in our exasperating situation.

"You look so funny, Elizabeth."

"Oh! *Ja*, you do, too. I guess we better get some more water."

"*Ja*, let's try it again."

We both went down the hill, laughing on our way to fetch another pail of water while repeating the Jack and Jill rhyme. Sometimes it's easier to do something when you joke about it rather than get angry.

We carried water morning and night. We needed several buckets for drinking and cooking, for washing faces and hands, and for the garbage buckets, which later were sent to the hogs. If any buckets ran low, we'd have to go out again. When it came time for bathing, that was another problem. Our West Virginia tub (a round galvanized tub) held six buckets. We took baths one night a week. With eight to ten people bathing, we had a beaten path between the pump and the house.

Inside, on those cold nights it was so quiet that any noise seemed magnified. No wonder we were startled when we heard the sound of an engine. We lived pretty far out in the

118

country and didn't get too many cars. Outside of the mailman's truck, we saw one or maybe two cars a week. That usually was the modern farmer who lived nearby.

The sound on this snowy night turned out to be that of a snowplow. It wasn't a very big one. The snow had a pretty big head start and was too much for the small plow to handle. It got stuck. A while later, a jumbo snowplow came along and pulled out the small plow.

"Never send a boy to do a man's job," mused Mother.

However, the next morning the older boys found the snow so deep, they couldn't get to the barn without using shovels first. They had to dig a tunnel to the barn so they could milk the cows. Although this was a practical and necessary task for the older boys, we younger children got a lot of fun out of the tunnel. Our first impression was, "Oh! How neat!"

"It's warm," we said.

"Just like the Eskimos," William spoke up.

"Watcha mean?"

"There are people that live in snow huts in Alaska."

"Oh, yeah? What do they eat?"

"You go get ready for school; you ask too many questions now."

When we walked to school that morning, we looked up on both sides of the road. All we could see was snowbanks, with a telephone line about three feet above the banks running to the modern farmer's house, and the blue sky.

We had cold weather along with that snow. Sometimes the temperature plunged below zero, once thirty-eight degrees below. Still, life went on. We just put on more clothing than usual. We had our long johns, heavy woolen capes for the girls, and bonnets, mittens, scarves, and shawls for the older girls and women. The boys had their heavy capes and earmuffs, too. Everything was in black material, as tradition dictated.

It was a dry cold, and we got used to it. When winter set in, it would stay cold until springtime. There would be snow on top of snow. After a snow had passed, the sun would come out and melt some, yet when night set in, the temperature would plunge back below freezing and leave a crispy crust on top of the tunnels of snow. We would walk with care on the high snowbanks on our way to and from school.

The Saturday following the first big snow, the boys took the old wagon's wheels off and put the sled runners on it. Wooden benches for us to sit on were placed in the wagon. The sled was a lot warmer than the buggy. Sunday morning, we all readied ourselves for church. We climbed into the box sled, which was covered with a canvas to keep us from getting frostbite in the bitter cold.

We weren't allowed to have a storm window on the buggy. This was one of the man-made traditions for our congregation. Their idea was if it's too cold for the people, it's too cold for the horses.

Since the Amish have church only on every other Sunday, the boys took advantage of their off-Sundays. When chores and breakfast were completed by 8:00 A.M., the boys dressed warmly and announced, "We are going ice-skating. The river is frozen solid, so we plan to skate down it. Two other farmer boys are going to meet us at the river at their homestead. We'll be back in time to do evening chores."

"Are you sure the river is solid?" Mother questioned.

"Oh, yeah. We took the ax down and checked to see how deep it's frozen," William answered.

"How deep is it?"

"It's eight to twelve inches, Mom. Nothing to worry about. It's hard all across that river."

"All right, just make sure it's safe. Watch the spots for rapids where it may not be solid."

"We'll be careful and don't worry. Bye."

"Have fun."

During the day, the other children got out their home-made wooden sled and double-bladed ice-skates. They did some sledding and took turns with one pair of iceskates. The skates were adjusted to each child's foot size and clamped to the shoes.

When it was time to do the evening chores, the boys were home. At the dinner table, the boys narrated the events of their exciting day. We all listened in silence as they recounted their adventures.

"We skated down the river, and our friends joined us when we got to their boundary line. When everybody had joined us as planned, we made a couple of safety rules. William is the oldest, so he took the lead. A single file was maintained to keep a safe distance in case the ice might break. We decided to skate one way till noon, then make a turn and come back."

"That really was fun," William interrupted.

"We could skate as fast as we wanted," Levi continued. "The whole river was all ours. We wanted to see just how far we could skate in a day. We didn't let no grass grow under us."

"Since I had the lead, I went as fast as I could. A couple of times when the ice cracked I leaped across and yelled back, 'soft spot!' Everybody followed with a leap. At noon we arrived in Fairbank. Fairbank is eight miles from here if you take the road. There were a couple of spots where the river had rapids and it wasn't frozen hard. But it was totally exciting, trying to beat the soft ice in different places like that."

Monday evening, the boys did their chores and after dinner took their beloved skates in their hands and headed for the river. The boys knew what the river was like to Fairbank, but they wanted to investigate in the opposite direction, to Littleton, too.

When the boys came home, they were all excited.

"Mom, guess what's happening in Littleton?" Levi asked.

"I have no idea. What is happening?"

"Some people are ice fishing. They've got a tractor with a blade on it to scrape the snow off the river. Then they took an ax to open the river. They drag a net to lift the fish out."

The young ones were curious. "What are they doing that for?" one asked.

121

"Because the river is frozen so hard, no air can get to the fish. The fish will die this year because of lack of oxygen. So we gave them a hand. The men said if the fish die, it will cause bigger floods. We can have all the fish that we want," Levi stated.

"May we drive the horse and buggy to Littleton to get some?" both boys asked. "We told them that we couldn't take fish with us on our ice-skates."

"Sure! Go get them if they said you may have them."

The boys left in their horse and buggy with a feed bag. They returned with a bagful of fish.

We ate fish for breakfast, lunch, and dinner until they were gone. Those fish were good eating while they lasted. Mother said, "Fish and rice are brain food." So we ate plenty of fish hoping it would make us smart.

At the breakfast table, William revealed his wish. "I hope what we did will keep the river from flooding in the spring." Everybody had to agree.

Levi's Disappearance

One Sunday in the spring of 1951, the sun was beaming down on the snow, causing it to disappear. As the snow melted, the creeks began to rise and rush into the river. The river rose over its banks, through the woods, and onto the tillable fields. The creek that ran behind the pigpen, chicken house, and outhouse passed along the garden and emptied into the wide river below. The creek rose to the garden. The river rose until it met the creek. The river was one-fourth of a mile from the house.

Every spring we had floods. The rising river would rush over our land, taking soil with it and covering the land with sand.

This Sunday morning, it was church Sunday. The Amish community had been wanting my brother Levi to join the church. To join the Amish church, a young boy or girl would have to go to a private room with the preacher for conferences on six church days. He or she would be taught the church rules and the church dress code. Then he or she would be baptized to become a member. Baptism was done by pouring water on the person's head.

Levi was getting ready for church. Mother and the younger children all readied themselves for church, too. We had to use two buggies to take our large family to church. Levi stated, "The bridges will be so flooded that we may never get across."

"Which way are you going?" Mother asked.

"I'm going to Littleton, across that bridge, because that one will be the last one to flood."

"We are going the other way," said Mother.

Mother, myself, and the younger children departed in our large family buggy with a team of horses. Before we arrived at the bridge, we came to a line of six buggies and a car at a standstill. We pulled up beside another buggy and asked, "What is the holdup?"

"Two boys are caught in the high water," they answered. The people in the car were upset and angry. "Those boys treated their horse terrible. They should be turned in for mistreating an animal. The two boys tried to cross the bridge, since the water was only about four inches over the bridge. They had a young horse barely broken for their single buggy."

We couldn't see because of the bend in the road and the woods, so we pulled our rig up along the left side of the traffic, near the bridge, on the high part of the land. We stopped. The water was rising and rushing down the river, overflowing its banks and covering woods, driveways, and tillable lowland fields.

From this vantage point we could see the two boys. The boys had thought they could enter the driveway of the farm right beyond the bridge. They were halfway in the driveway when the water arrived so high and so fast that it reached the box of the buggy and went above the horse's stomach. The young horse was frightened and didn't want to move any farther, so it came to a complete stop. The boys stepped down into waist-high water. One boy tied the buggy to the fence post so it wouldn't be washed down the river. The other one unhitched the horse and coaxed it away from the buggy. The boys, one after the other, jumped on the horse's back and rode it to the homestead.

We watched until they arrived on high ground. Then all the people in line took turns turning around and returned to their homes in safety. When we arrived home, we didn't see Levi, so we thought he had made it across the bridge. When evening set in, we did our chores, but he still didn't come home.

A friend, David, stopped and asked, "Is Levi all right?"

Mother explained what happened that morning and told him Levi had taken the other road to church.

"Levi wasn't in church."

"He wasn't?"

Mother was worried now. She looked at Brother William and told him, "Go to Littleton to see if that bridge is flooded."

William was worried, too, and concerned for Levi. He promptly agreed to check the bridge. David left with these last words: "If you need help with anything, let me know."

"Thank you."

William hitched up the horse and buggy and left to check the Littleton bridge. We had all lost our appetite for dinner, wondering where Levi was and what had happened to him. We waited and hoped William would find some answers about Levi. William returned home and had no idea where Levi was, saying, "This is a puzzle! The people in Littleton said that the river didn't overflow the bridge until noon. But that gave him plenty of time to get across before it overflowed."

It was dark, but we waited until eleven o'clock. Then we all went to bed and hoped that Levi would return before morning.

At daybreak, everybody went to check to see if Levi had returned home during the night. What a disappointment! No Levi! We did our morning chores, and then we gathered at the table to eat. One of my sisters, Susan, stated, "Mom, you have one too many place settings."

"Susan, go out and call Levi in for breakfast," my mother said in a soft, concerned voice.

We all looked at each other and at Mom. Due to her worried appearance, we all obeyed with no arguments. We went to the table, except for Susan, who went outside to call Levi in.

The Amish families have a silent prayer before and after their meals. After prayer, we would all start reaching and pass the food around the table. This day, the meal was silent. Everybody still had questions and was worried. Why didn't Levi come home? Why call him before meals? We all ate our breakfast and then said our silent prayer before we were excused from the table.

After breakfast, Mother told William, "Go get the horse and buggy ready; we two are going to Littleton once more to double-check."

William agreed. Mother readied herself and they went to town, leaving the younger ones at home.

As they were going down the country road, we who were left at home went to the kitchen window to watch them. They disappeared over the rolling hills, and then we looked down at the high water where the creek and the river united, no land in sight.

How was this possible? But it was possible. We were looking at it. We learned at our young age not by someone telling us a story, but by seeing it with our own eyes. It was hard to believe that a river that is so calm in the summertime could grow to be as dangerous as a roaring lion.

This Monday morning, the sun was shining. Spring was here to stay. At about 11:00 A.M., Mom and William were returning home. We saw two buggies coming down the road. We all ran to meet them, yelling,"Levi's buggy's coming too!" We cheered, jumping and waiting for them to get to the house. However, as they pulled past the house into the driveway, the happy cheers ended. There was silence! Eyes were wide open with disbelief. Oh, no! Why? We saw William driving Levi's horse and buggy up to the homestead. We all went out to see them.

William unhitched the horse with a younger brother's help. Daniel, the younger brother, stated, "I see you found the horse and buggy. Where is Levi?"

"Don't know."

The girls asked, "Mom, where is Levi?"

"We don't know. The rig was in Littleton tied behind the gas station. William missed it last night."

We all were disappointed. Mother asked, "Susan, do you have dinner on?"

"Yes, it's on the stove."

We didn't feel like doing anything. Nobody did much, as on the first day of Levi's absence. We did our chores and that was about it.

For every meal, Levi was called, with a place setting on the table for him in his absence. Days had gone by and still there was no word from him or anybody of his disappearance.

Mother told us, "Life goes on and we have to continue."

Holmes County, Ohio

Shunning

After the high water had receded in the river and creek channels in the spring of 1951, their boundaries returned to normal. It was planting season and the garden and fields were being plowed and seeded. Everybody helped Mother and each other, because we were short one hand with Levi's absence.

Two weeks later, on a Sunday, the children did not go to church, thinking maybe Levi would come home. We weren't leaving home in case he did return. Levi didn't return. Four weeks passed; we wouldn't leave still, in hopes he might come home. That Sunday afternoon at around 4:00 P.M., the boys were getting ready to do the milking. We girls were getting dinner ready. We heard an engine down the road. We looked, but didn't recognize who it was. The car stopped in front of the house and took off again.

A voice yelled, "Levi's home! Levi's home!"

We were surprised and could hardly believe it. When I turned around from setting the table, he was standing there in person, dressed in a plaid shirt and blue jeans. He picked up the baby, and Annie ran to him. He swept her off her feet and hugged them both.

Junior ran and hugged Levi's leg, then decided that wasn't enough. Junior climbed up on the worktable and grabbed Levi around the neck to hug him. He just laughed; he had been homesick.

The other boys came running in from the barn to see their brother. Everybody wanted to talk to him at the same time. There was laughter in the home again. I stood back and enjoyed the rejoicing sight. I was relieved that Levi hadn't gotten caught in the high water. He was really alive.

Mother asked, "Are you hungry?"

"No. I'm not staying."

"Stay for dinner; we have a place set for you."

"No. My friend went to turn the car around, and then he'll be right back to pick me up."

Mother looked out the window and commented, "Oh! He parked in the driveway. I hope Uncle Judas doesn't see it."

"Why?"

"Because the Amish tradition here is when one leaves home or the church, he isn't supposed to park his car on the home place."

"What?"

"That's what they call shunning," William interrupted.

"Well, we have to go anyway."

Everybody pleaded, "Don't go; don't go."

"I'll be back again."

"When?" The young ones didn't want to let him go.

"I wanted you to know I'm all right and I'm working on a large farm about sixty miles from here, close to Waterloo."

"Come back and stay longer next time."

"All right, I will."

He left, but nobody was ready to see him go so soon. We were glad he was all right. His visit was a pleasant surprise.

I was relieved and said, "I'm glad he stopped to let us know he was okay." I realized then that Levi's leaving home was a reaction to the recent pressure on him to join the church.

Everyone went back to their duties again with relief. It was easier to do the chores now, but there was still sorrow because we missed him.

At the dinner table, I asked, "Why isn't Levi supposed to come home and park a car here?"

"Because he left home and he changed his dress code. He has his hair cut in a shingle," Mother answered.

"Well, I think he looks handsome."

Levi was five-nine, dark-haired, and well built for an eighteen-year-old boy.

"He really did look good," agreed Susan. "I don't understand why it's so wrong to have different colors in our clothes."

"Joseph in the Bible had so many brothers; they wore plain clothes, too. But they mistreated him. Yet the Bible teaches that Joseph had a coat of many colors and he was the good guy," Daniel commented. "Why don't the Amish believe in other colors then?"

Mother replied, "The Amish claim other colors are of the world. We are to look different from the world."

Although it would be hard to be the only ones making the change, the children weren't very happy with their traditions. These were man-made traditions.

On a Sunday two weeks later, Levi stopped in again. We all were just as happy to see him then as we were before. We went through the same exciting experience. This time his friend-whose name was Levi also, parked his car close to the bend down the road so we wouldn't get in trouble with the church.

"Levi, the people asked today if you were going to join the church," Mother stated.

"No, I'll never join the church here."

"Won't you come back home?"

"No. I've got a good job. I'm making eighty dollars a month, plus a place to stay. They are good to me, too."

"Stay for supper."

"No, I'd better get going before somebody comes through and sees the car."

No one wanted him to leave, but we were glad he had stopped by again.

"You will come back again, won't you?" Mother asked.

"Yeah! I'll be back." He kissed the young ones and left.

This time two weeks went by and he didn't stop back. A whole month passed before he stopped again.

Mother asked, "What could I do to get you to come back home?"

"I don't know. I'm not joining that church."

Levi stayed for a while, helping the boys with their chores, but he wouldn't stay for dinner. According to the local Amish tradition, Mother and Brother William were supposed to shun him. To "shun" means that they were not supposed to eat with him or have anything to do with him.

131

Still, Levi's plate was always set at the dinner table and his name was called before we sat down to eat.

On Levi's next visit home, Mother asked, "Would you like for us to move away from here?"

"Where would you want to move to?"

"Let me check with the uncles in Ohio."

"All right."

In August, he visited us again. Mother stated, "I received a letter from your uncle."

"*Ja*? And?"

"They said they would have a house for us and there are jobs available there."

"Watcha going to do with the farm?"

"We'll have an auction in the fall and rent the farm, then make our move."

"Sell everything?"

"We'll just take our personal belongings and a horse and buggy."

"Does everybody else want to go?"

"Oh, yeah!" we yelled.

"We're sick of these church people picking on everything we do," someone said.

The previous summer, the boys had met our neighbor across the river. He had an airplane and told the boys if they came over some Sunday he would take them for a ride. The boys told him they would hold him to that. On that following Sunday, we were invited to go to Uncle's house for dinner. The boys went over to see the farmer about the airplane, ride.

The neighbor took them for a ride in the sky. When the plane flew over Uncle's farm, we spotted it and waved to them. The plane signaled back and started to do some fancy tricks. Later in the afternoon when we arrived home, the boys were already doing their chores.

Everybody went to church the following Sunday. Before church started, it was announced that there would be a meeting for the members after the service. Alter the service, the children were excused and only the adults remained.

Somehow the people knew Brother William had taken an airplane ride. They wanted him to make a confession for taking that ride. He didn't think he did anything wrong. They told him they would expel him if he didn't make it right with the church. To keep peace in the community, he did what was demanded of him.

However, William was upset with the church over this issue. He could see no wrong in what he had done. When we came home from church, everyone was upset over the matter.

The younger ones were fast learning that the Amish ways in Buchanan County, Iowa, were not in harmony with ours.

Not only that, Brother Levi wasn't coming back to stay as long as we lived there. Mother made arrangements to have an auction in November of 1951. When she made the announcement, oh, how the church members tried to talk her out of it! Having Levi back home with us again was more important to Mother than what the people felt about us making the change.

Levi had quit his job a month before the auction to help us get ready for the big day. He didn't worry about his dress code, and Mother didn't put pressure on him. It was great to have Levi fill the empty place at the table, and we didn't worry about the tradition of shunning.

Beware lest any man spoil you through
philosophy and vain deceit after the tradition of
men, after the rudiments of the world,
not after Christ.
Colossians 2:8

133

Berne, Indiana

Leaving Iowa

In November of 1951, the auction day was nearing. Everyone was excitedly running around to get ready for the big day. The girls helped package the household goods.

The boys, working in harmony, asked Mother, "Where do you want the machinery parked? What do we pack to take along to Ohio? Which horse do we take to Ohio? How are we going to handle the animals at the auction?"

Mother discussed it with the boys. "The farm equipment has to be parked close to the barn in a neat row. We'll take the hand tools to Ohio in a toolbox."

"Which horse do you want to take along?" she asked the boys.

"I want to take Esther," Levi said.

"No, I want to take my horse," William stated.

Each boy had a good horse and didn't want to part with it. Mother decided that they both could go along. The horse Junior had taught all the tricks had to be sold, and so did the draft horses.

Levi stated, "The animals can't be parked in a row. How are we going to auction them off?"

"We'll have to leave everything in the barn, and when the auctioneer is ready for the animals, you boys will have to bring one animal out at a time so the people can see what is for sale."

Mother knew another Amish family that wanted to rent the farm. Uncle Judas wanted to get the rental agreement together for the renters, for Mother, and for Father's new guardian, a banker in Independence, who would be collecting the rent for us.

Uncle Judas wanted Mother to buy the fertilizer for the renters. Mother said, "Do you think I'm going to buy fertilizer for the renters after you refused to let me fertilize those fields while I was farming? I won't even think of it."

"Those fields need to be fertilized," Uncle Judas said.

"That's what I've been trying to tell you for several years, but you always told me they didn't need it. Now that I'm moving out, they need it, but for all I care, you can buy the fertilizer yourself. I knew those fields needed fertilizer for years!"

Since we were leaving Iowa, arrangements had been made making a banker in Independence Father's new guardian. When that was done, Mother said to the banker, "Judas has taken all the money. Shouldn't I be entitled to get half since I'm the wife?"

"Didn't you get half?"

"No, I didn't get any of it."

"What did you live on then?"

Mother explained what and how we lived. The banker could hardly believe it and was shaking his head. "Your brother did that to his own sister and children?" he questioned.

"Yeah." The banker made arrangements to get Mother's share for her.

Mother decided to move our personal belongings and household goods in a moving van. The family would travel to Ohio in a hired three-seater automobile, driven by a man none of us knew. The day after the auction, Mother was disappointed. The sale didn't bring in much money for everything that was sold. Of course, Uncle Judas was right there to take the money on auction day. Early that morning, everyone in our family was up, loading the semi-truck and getting ready to leave for Ohio.

Before we left, we learned that Uncle Judas refused to give Mother her money. He was going with us to Ohio to personally deliver Mother's money to Uncle Levi Troyer. Mother didn't argue with him. We children were packed in the automobile like sardines. The middle seat didn't have a back, which made the trip uncomfortable. Uncle Judas sat up front with the driver. We thought if our uncle hadn't come with us, it would've been a more comfortable trip. But we really didn't mind, because we were moving away from an unhappy period of our life, one that I really believed none of us would ever be able to forget. I was scared, not knowing what was ahead for us.

It was an eighteen hour trip to Ohio. We arrived at Uncle Levi's homestead early in the morning on the day before Thanksgiving. Uncle Levi and Aunt Esther were just getting ready to do their morning chores when we arrived. Aunt Esther was happy to see us and welcomed us all to the house. She asked us if we wanted to go to bed.

We all nodded our heads, and Mother said, "I'm tired, but I don't think I could sleep right now."

We all were tired, but too excited to crawl in bed at that moment. Then Esther asked, "Where's William and Levi?"

"The boys are coming with the moving van. It's taking them longer because they have to stop to exercise their horses on the way."

"Would you like to have breakfast? I'll make breakfast now," Aunt Esther offered.

"No, we'll wait until the chores are done and eat breakfast with you," Mother replied.

Glancing around Aunt Esther's kitchen, I saw a green dress hanging up beside the stairway. I just stood there and looked at it.

Aunt Esther saw me and said, "Do you recognize that dress?"

"Is that the dress that Mom made me?"

Aunt Esther walked over and lifted the dress off the hook, saying, "*Ja*, this is the dress your mother made for you."

"Are we allowed to have that kind of dress here?"

"You sure may," she said, hanging the dress back up.

Then I suddenly realized the move to Ohio was a good move and it would be different now. I was sure it was for the better, even though we hated to leave Dad behind.

"Aunt Esther, is there anything we can do to help with chores or breakfast?" we asked.

As we were helping her, we visited. While we were visiting, one of my sisters whispered, "Did you see Uncle

137

Judas sitting at the doorway trying to listen to our conversation?"

Aunt Esther shook her head and stated, "*Ja*, he's eavesdropping."

He's trying to hear what we have to say and probably doesn't approve," Mom replied.

"Well, we aren't saying anything that we have to hide," Aunt Esther commented, laughing.

While they were talking, I looked over and saw Uncle Judas sitting there listening. I could hardly believe it. As I was looking at him, a vision flashed through my head. I don't believe anyone saw the light except for myself. The light blocked the surroundings from me momentarily. It was as if a voice were saying, *Write a book about Iowa.*

I asked, *A book?*

Yes, write a book about your life in Iowa.

Oh, but I don't know how to even begin.

You will in time, and the voice left me.

I could never forget that moment, and I've asked myself over and over again, *Why am I supposed to write this book? Why me?* It came to be an obsession with me.

I had to write this book, even if it's against my family's wishes.

Epilogue

Today Brother William is a married farmer. He and his wife have ten children. Brother Levi is married and has his own buggy shop. He and his wife have ten children. Sister Susan is married to a factory employee. They have three children. They are foster parents for the county. Sister Polly died. Brother Daniel is a married farmer, and he and his wife have five children. Sister Alma, the author, is divorced and has three children. Sister Elizabeth is married to a man who is a carpenter and a farmer. They have four children. Junior is married. He has seven children and is a truck driver. Sister Anne is married. Her husband rebuilds automobiles. She makes Amish dolls. They have five children. Joseph Jay was the baby when we left Iowa. He is married and has three children. He is an assistant manager for a major department store. We are living in Ohio except for Junior. Junior has his residence in Pennsylvania.

Alma Hershberger has compiled Alma's Amish Kitchen Cookbook (with over 500 recipes), The Alphabet in Amish Life (a child's book), and Art of Amish Cooking (with 650 recipes). Annie's handmade Amish dolls are like the ones that pioneer children played with. They are seventeen inches long, washable, and come in boy or girl versions. For information on ordering dolls or cookbooks, please write: Art of Amish Taste, P.O. Box 375, Danville, OH 43014.

Intercourse, Pennsylvania

Kalona, Iowa

Berne, Indiana

AMISH TASTE
BOX 375
DANVILLE, OHIO 43014

Please send the following:

AMISH TASTE COOKING STEP by STEP $4.95
ART OF AMISH COOKING (650 Recipes)..........$10.95
ALMA'S AMISH KITCHEN (532 Recipes)..........$10.95
AMISH LIFE THROUGH A CHILD'S EYES*......$6.95
*A rare true story about an Amish family, published in paperback.
AMISH WOMEN...$5.95
AMISH DOLL (Girl 17") Each.............................$26.95
AMISH DOLL (Boy 17") Pair $48.95

Please add postage and packaging
cost for dolls (Shipping U.P.S.) $3.35
Plus add Postage $2.40, for 1st book and $1.00
for each additional book ...._____
Ohio Residents sales tax 5-1/2% ...._____

NAME: _____ DATE: _____

STREET/BOX: _____

CITY: _____ STATE:_____ ZIP: _____

TELEPHONE #: _____

No C.O.D.'s Please

QUANTITY	ITEM	PRICE
_____ *	_____	=$ _____
_____ *	_____	=$ _____
_____ *	_____	=$ _____
_____ *	_____	=$ _____
_____ *	_____	=$ _____

Packaging for Dolls: ....=$ _____
Postage for Books: ....=$ _____
Sales Tax if Applicable: ....=$ _____
Total Amount Paid: ....=$ _____

Looking for a *Fund Raising Project.* The Author loves to help groups like yours. She has helped others and is willing to help you Cook up a *Fundraising Success.*
Just fill in the form below and mail it.

AMISH TASTE COOKING - STEP by STEP
ATTENTION: ALMA
ART OF AMISH TASTE
P.O. BOX 375
DANVILLE, OHIO 43014-0375

Our Organization is interested in Cooking up a *Fundraiser Project.* Please mail us more information.

Organization Name: _____

Leader's Name: _____

Address: _____

City: _____ State: _____

Zip Code: _____ _____ Date: _____

COMMENTS: _____
_____
_____
_____
_____
_____
_____
_____
_____
_____
_____